TIBERIUS CAESAR

TIBERIUS CAESAR

BY FERDINAND DUGUE

*Translated and adapted
by Frank J. Morlock*

WILDSIDE PRESS

Copyright © 2010 by Frank J. Morlock

Published by Wildside Press LLC.
www.wildsidebooks.com

CHARACTERS

TIBERIUS, Emperor
CAIUS CALIGULA
PROCULA VINDEX
ROMULUS, Citizen of Rome
NERVA
AURELIUS
PORCIUS
AENEAS
EVANDRE
NATALIS
SENECA, Philosopher
NARSES
ALBIN
BROGITAR
A PRAETORIAN
A DOCTOR
AN EXECUTIONER
THREE DRUIDS
KIOMARA, Gallic Slave Girl
BLANDINE, Daughter of Nerva
CHARICLEA, Blandine's Nurse
PATRICIANS, SOLDIERS, SLAVES, GLADIATORS, DANCERS, PRAETORIANS, ETC.

ACT I

SCENE I: THE REVOLTERS

A square in the Carenes suburb of Rome. To the right, the palace of Nerva. To the left, the shop of the armourer Procula.

Streets and monuments in perspective.

PROCULA

It's getting late. Hasten to carry these weapons to the patrician's who ordered them from me.

(to a worker)

You know the dwelling of Senator Fonteius. Deliver to him, on my behalf this sword and military belt.

(to another)

You will go to Lord Atalus on the Flaminnian Way, turning right, toward the Palatine.

(to a third)

You to the home of the Tribune Lemas who dwells in that magnificent house with jets of water and huge cedars, down there on the other side of the golden column.

Get going and don't lose a moment! Ah, I was forgetting, there's still one more cuirass to take to the home of the illustrious Natalis, the former Consul.

NATALIS (entering)

Lower, will you, much lower—are you losing your wits to raise your voice that way on an open street?

PROCULA

May the Gods protect you, Lord Natalis. I was sending you your cuirass.

NATALIS

It's unnecessary. I will try it on at your place.

PROCULA

As you please.

(to others)

The rest of you, leave.

NATALIS

Will you hide those weapons under your tunics. Do you need to allow passers-by to see what you are carrying?

PROCULA

Where's the harm? The passers-by would say: Here are very shiny well chiseled blades. They would conclude it came from the armourer Procula. My pride would find its count.

NATALIS (lowering his voice)

Tiberius doesn't like this sort of merchandise circulating too freely in Rome.

PROCULA

Eh, Lord? What do I have to fear from Tiberius? I am an artisan who makes weapons without inquiring the use they are intended for. As I hold nothing in the state, nothing that takes place in Rome can concern me, so long as it is not a question of Lord Nerva, my protector, my master.

NATALIS

Well, it's in his name that I ask you today to use prudence.

PROCULA

In that case it's a different matter.

(lowering his voice to a worker)

Separate from them now. Don't allow a skin of steel under your tunic to appear, and take the most deserted streets.

(workers leave.)

Would you like to try on your cuirass now, Lord?

NATALIS

You guarantee me that it is dagger proof?

PROCULA

Completely.

NATALIS

Fine. You'll fit it on me yourself. I'll keep it under my pallium.

PROCULA

Order, Lord.

(aside)

Let's rid ourselves quickly of this patrician because now's the hour she emerges every evening.

(They go into the shop. A group of Patricians approaches.)

PORCIUS

Coe on, my dear Evander, there's no going back.

EVANDRE

Success isn't doubtful.

PORCIUS

Thus it's quite certain that Tiberius has no suspicion, that he hasn't left for Capri.

EVANDRE

Nerva affirmed it to me less than an hour ago.

PORCIUS

And the Praetorian Guard is with us?

EVANDRE

Caligula himself must bring it over to us.

PORCIUS

Caligula, the nephew of Tiberius, his heir? Humph! I really fear—

EVANDRE

What? The child is in a hurry to reign. That's natural.

PORCIUS

Indeed, it's true—but, between ourselves, the augurs are not favorable. I had the sacred chicken shut in its cage and it refused to eat.

EVANDRE

Because it wasn't hungry.

PORCIUS

You jest, impious one that you are? Will you still laugh if I tell you that this morning, by mistake, I put on my left boot before my right?

EVANDRE

Presaging misfortune and death.

PORCIUS

That was the opinion of the great Augustus and it's mine?

EVANDRE

Decidedly, my old Procius, fear will turn your head.

(going to meet other patricians who enter)

Be welcome, Seneca, long life to you Numa, your hand Aeneas. —Any news?

AENEAS

Everything is going beautifully. I left Caligula. Together we visited the barracks on the Palatine Hill.

EVANDRE

And it's still this way that the cadaver of Plautus will be dragged to the pillory.?

AENEAS

Still.

PORCIUS

That brave Plautus! That excellent Plautus! When I think that yesterday I supped with him. You know he had the most admirable cooks in the world for dormouse in poppy juice. Poor friend! And for benjoin sauce. —Generous colleague! Without mentioning that Falernian of 100 leaves which dated from his ancestor Opimius! We emerged from his palace staggering a bit. He forgot to bow his head in passing a statue of Tiberius—the freedman of an informer saw him and this morning he was found dead in his bed. P Plautu, o best of men, to think that we will no longer drink together.

SENECA

Silence, Porcius! To think of his bowels when it's a question of saving the country—it's indecent!

PORCIUS

Right! Now here's Seneca preaching abstinence. But why do you scorn wine and good cheer?

SENECA

Because I am a philosopher.

PORCIUS

Come off it. Because you have bad digestion!

EVANDER

There, there—no quarreling, I beg you. It's necessary to avenge Plautus.

PORCIUS

Yes! But the people? Are you sure of the populace?

SENECA

I will harangue them.

PORCIUS (aside)

This scrawny philosopher is good only for making phrases.

(Natalis emerges from Procula's shop.)

AENEAS

Ha! Here's Natalis.

NATALIS

Imprudents that you are. Don't stand around in groups like this in this square, Let's go into Nerva's.

ALL:

Let's go in.

AURELIUS

Halt right there my noble friends.

EVANDER

What does this bone head of an Aurelius want with us?

NATALIS (low)

Let's avoid him.

(aloud)

Evening Aurelius, Evening. We are expected somewhere.

AURELIUS

Stay put, I tell you.

NATALIS

But—

AURELIUS

You are conspiring. Very good. I'm one of you.

EVANDER

Are you drunk?

AURELIUS

No. Unfortunately, I cannot even get high.

PORCIUS (aside)

Poor man!

AURELIUS

So you are conspiring, right? I'm with you. Oh, first of all ff you don't want me, I'll denounce you. It's true, it's already been done, no question.

PORCIUS

Huh?

AURELIUS

To conspire under old Tiberius without being denounced,—why, that would be a prodigy, since even those who do not conspire are denounced! Aren't there informers everywhere? In the friend that embraces you, in the woman you love, in the air that goes by, in the flowers that bloom, in the tomb that closes?

EVANDER

Shut up, wretch, shut up!

AURELIUS

Not at all, at all. By all the Gods of Hell, I will say all I have to say. I have a flux of eloquence like the philosopher Seneca.

NATALIS

But you intend to ruin us!

AURELIUS

I'm ruining myself with you.

PORCIUS

Ah, the mad man!

AURELIUS

Informers everywhere, always informers! I knew a son who denounced his father; a sister, her brother; a wife, her husband—my right hand will denounce my left! Raise your eyes to heaven—it's a crime, be out or come in, laugh or weep, be serious or distracted, active or idle, walk, run, listen, reply, cough too loud, blow your nose in a certain way—all that's a crime ! The informer is there. Roman, he must die—Tiberius insists on it. Tiberius will have you butchered by a soldier, strangled by an executioner, or bled by a surgeon! In a mood of clemency, he invites you politely to suicide or to taste some of his delicious food. May the Gods preserve you from the parties of Tiberius!

EVANDER

Luckily, this place is deserted.

AURELIUS

That's where Rome is, my good friends! And to say I'm still alive. By Jupiter, it's cause for despair! I thought aloud, I publicly insulted Tiberius, I trod hi image under my feet, as I do again, the one that I wear on my finger! Well, I've never had the luck to be denounced. There are informers for everybody but me. It makes you think that in the end they don't take you seriously. Still, I can't yet denounce myself! Nevertheless, I've decided, weary of war, since Ihad a good idea. Let's conspire. I said to myself, it's the best way to get it over with quickly. And so, here I am! Well, where are we, my good friends? Put me au courant. I'm all ears.

NATALIS

This is dementia.

AURELIUS

Not at all. Let's consider it a little. Each of you here has a motive for conspiring. I have the right to mine. Porcius conspires from fear. Evander because he is ruined. You, because you want to be Consul again. Seneca because—actually, why is he conspiring?

SENECA

Because I am a philosopher.

AURELIUS

And bilious. Me, I conspire because I am weary of life. It's a sort of suicide I intend to make fashionable! Opening one's veins in a bath has become too common. I've got a better way. With the lancet, the dagger, poison, asphyxiation, drowning one may miss his mark—which is a bore. You must start all over again and that's tiresome. While conspiring with you, one is sure of one's fate.

NATALIS

Why shut up, will you!

PORCIUS

At least speak lower.

AURELIUS

To wake up, to go to sleep, be cold, be hot, hang around with drunks like Porcius, and philosophers like Seneca, go by foot or in a letter, and start all over again every day—is there anything more insipid? I bear one of the greatest names in Rome; I'm one of the Julian house which has on one side, Clodius, the Sabine, and Aeneas, King of Alba on the other. I've led the most extravagant and dissipated life; I've had mistresses by the hundreds, friends by the thousands, and despite my lunacy, my prodigality, my follies, I've never been able to devour my enormous inheritance—which infuriates me; in short, at thirty years of age, I'm disgusted by everything completely bored, radically blasé; I hold in honor the two best things in the world, young love and old wine; I can no longer love or drink—my heart has gastritis like my stomach. You see plainly, the moment has come for me to conspire against old Tiberius.

NATALIS

Well, so be it! We will make room for you if Nerva wants you.

AURELIUS (becoming serious)

Nerva! Noble heart, pure life, old fashioned character—we are a band of ambitious men and good-for-nothings. Nerva alone is a man! Come on, will you, you will see how under such a leader this fool, this debauched Aurelius, Faces Peril and death!

NATALIS

Let's not all go through the main gate. Let Aeneas and two or three others enter by way of the garden.

AURELIUS (very gaily)

I think that this time, for sure, I don't have long to live.

(They all leave)

PROCULUS

Yet another conspiracy. More work for the executioners of Tiberius.

(looking toward Nerva's palace)

May thunder at least spare that house! Here's your day over, poor artisan. Rest your weary eyes by the chimney of the workshop. Come savor a moment of air passing through these trees. Especially come, motionless, silently, dazzled—admirer of the shining vision which fills your thoughts and burns your heart. Will the young patrician emerge tonight?

(Romulus enters joyfully and strikes him on the shoulder.)

ROMULUS

Good evening, Barbarian!

PROCULUS

Ah!

(getting hold of himself)

Good evening, friend Romulus.

ROMULUS

Your friend. Still, it's true. To say that I, Romulus, Citizen of Rome, I, who descend directly from Pasiphae, the Mother of the Minotaur, am the friend of a Barbarian—

PROCULUS

You, you stoop—?

ROMULUS

Ah, so much the worse! I am not proud and I give you my hand willingly.

PROCULUS

And I shake it the same way.

ROMULUS

Poor Procula! Truly, you are not humiliated by your condition? Thus, you don't even know where you were born; you are not sure if you are a Gaul, a German or a Spaniard?

PROCULUS

I don't know. The secret of my birth belongs to Lord Nerva, who raised me with his slaves.

PROCULUS

And you've never asked him this secret?

PROCULUS

Never. He's been good to me; as a child he let me open his books, admire his paintings, his statues, his mosaics; later he had me taught a trade, he gave me this shop at the gate of his palace. May the Gods reward him for it.

ROMULUS

To be a slave; to know nothing more.

PROCULUS

I know that I have a love, and that's enough for me.

ROMULUS

To be freed so as to have to work to live!

PROCULUS

Work is a beautiful and holy thing which purifies the heart often and always raises it.

ROMULUS

For goodness sakes! Work degrades man! Is it possible not to be shamed by dirtying one's hands handling tools? Scorn industry and commerce for those who, like me, have the honor of being citizens of Rome. It's up to their Caesar to nourish them.

PROCULUS

Not very. I am furious with Tiberius!

PROCULUS

Truly!

ROMULUS

Tiberius is an old miser who doesn't give the least largesse to the people of Rome. Would you believe it, it's reached the point that I don't have a copper in my pocket? I still need a little to purchase a new tunic.

PROCULUS (smiling)

Indeed.

ROMULUS

Moreover, I rented a room on the eighth floor in a suburb. The house was very ugly and the street very smelly. At night, you could hear the songs of singers and the howling of dogs. I was surrounded by whores, little Greeks, unemployed grammarians, beggars who spoiled sheep with garlic. I have for a neighbor a mountebank who contrived to cripple a little girl to make tours on the Sublicius bridge. In short, I was horribly bad, but I have simple tastes, and I contented myself with this modest support when my landlord, an Israelite merchant put me out the door—me, a citizen of Rome, because I hadn't paid my rent. Now that's what happens friend, under the reign of Tiberius.

PROCULUS

Ah, it's intolerable!

ROMULUS

You laugh, yes, but I am very serious and will end by making Tiberius repent of his avarice. Because we are all powerful, the rest of us, the Citizens of Rome; it's for us to enjoy everything without paying for anything! The Aediles owe us games, Triumphs, money; the Magistrates, wheat; when one is noble or knight they mock the little folk, these men in tunics, but come election day, these fine gentlemen all us by our names, press our hands, buy our votes; the Tribunes pay court to us, and the Caesars care for us. Thus we are like three hundred thousand stockholders at the expense of the state in the city of Rome.

Do you imagine that, on the day we get angry, Tiberius won't tremble in all his members?

PROCULUS

Friend, forget Tiberius who is stronger.

ROMULUS

As for me, I intend that he pay his debts. Augustus bequeathed to the Roman people 45 million sesterces in his will. Tiberius, his heir still owes them to us.

(Procula turns and notices Kiomara, who stops with an old geezer she's leading.)

PROCULUS (pointing her out to Romulus)

Silence.

(Kiomara and the old man leave.)

ROMULUS

What's wrong with you? There you are, troubled by two passers-by, crossing the square.

PROCULUS (lowering his voice)

Heavens, one more time: forget Tiberius and find another means to fill your empty pocket.

ROMULUS

Such as?

PROCULUS

Work for me as an apprentice.

ROMULUS

Hammers, filings, the stench of copper. Yuck! Won't you ever understand the dignity of a Roman Citizen?

PROCULUS

Then let me loan you some money.

ROMULUS

To borrow from the purse of a barbarian!

PROCULUS

From that of a friend.

ROMULUS

My friendship doesn't go that far.

PROCULUS

All the same—

ROMULUS

Don't insist—you'll insult me.

PROCULUS

At your ease, ragamuffin Lord.

PROCULUS

I am no less grateful, my dear friend. But, I'm not worried, go. Jupiter, who protects me, will end by sending me some good windfall.

(Nerva emerges from his palace with Blandine and Chariclea.)

PROCULUS

Shut up!

NERVA

Blandine, my cherished daughter, go pray to the Gods of Rome that they render Rome glorious.

BLANDINE (aside)

The Gods of Rome!

NERVA (low to Chariclea)

Chariclea, you are taking her to the Temple of Vesta, aren't you?

CHARICLEA

Yes, master.

NERVA (low)

The Temple is the place of asylum, and as it's possible there may be tumult in the city—don't leave it. I will come to get you myself. You quite understand me—and you will obey?

CHARICLEA

Yes, Lord.

NERVA (to Blandine)

Hug me one more. Till soon, dear daughter. I love you with the tenderness of a mother.

(aside)

In a few moments, she'll be safe. Now that you no longer have to tremble for her, to work, old Roman.

(returns to his palace.)

BLANDINE (low to Chariclea)

Ah, good nurse—it's frightful to deceive one's father like this. When will I be able to tell him everything?

CHARICLEA

Patience, my child. It's one of those pious fibs that heaven pardons. But, how will we do it? Your father believes we are going to the Temple of Vesta, and forbids us to leave because there might be some tumult in Rome.

BLANDINE

A danger threatens him, perhaps. Oh—my place is beside him. I'm staying.

CHARICLEA

Blandine, it's the hour that the holy old man is waiting for us.

BLANDINE

Let's leave then. But, we'll return quickly.

(They both leave)

PROCULA

Not even the alms of a look. It's all very simple—a slave.

ROMULUS (picking up something)

I was telling you that Jupiter would come to my rescue. Now, here I am, rich!

(Kiomara and the old geezer re-appear.)

All I have to do is run to sell this at the goldsmith's.

PROCULA

What are you talking about?

ROMULUS

This gewgaw that I just picked up, and that one of those women doubtless lost.

PROCULA

Give me that.

ROMULUS

A joke of a jewe. It's made in the form of a ross. The silver seems fine.

PROCULA

Yes, I remember. The daughter of Nerva wore that object on her neck. I've noticed it several times.

ROMULUS

It's an amulet that doubtless she must have brought back from Jerusalem where her father was Questor: it seems these Jews are completely idolatrous and pagans.

PROCULA (aside)

O good luck! I might be able to approach her, to speak to her.

(He grabs the jewel)

ROMULUS

Well! What are you doing?

PROCULA

I'm placing the jewel in my belt until I can return it to her.

ROMULUS

Return it? What are you thinking of? I need money.

KIOMARA (coming up)

Would you like to earn a gold-piece?

ROMULUS

Huh?

KIOMARA

I'm asking you if you'd like to earn a gold coin.

ROMULUS

By working?

KIOMARA

No—that would be unworthy of a Citizen of Rome.

ROMULUS

You know who I am?

KIOMARA

I know it.

ROMULUS (aside)

Decidedly, I'm well known.

(aloud)

And what must be done?

KIOMARA

A small thing. I dwell far from this quarter—on the other side of the Pomerium, and I left there this morning with my father who is blind. The old man is weary of the trip and it's necessary to keep him here until my return

ROMULUS

That's easy. But I see from that ring that you are a slave. How is it that you have gold to spend?

KIOMARA

I'm not paying you to question me. Do you accept, yes or no?

ROMULUS

I accept, but you are going to find some gallant. It's easy to have a blind father, and if you will, my beautiful girl,—

(he takes her by the waist and she abruptly pushes him away.)

What looks! One would say the eyes of a panther.

KIOMARA (low to the old man)

You'll be fine here.

(aside)

Let's run to save the imprudent youth who will ruins himself without me.

(she leaves)

ROMULUS

O Decadence! Here I am a blind man's dog now. An idea, Procula, let's make a swap. I will leave you the silver gewgaw, and you watch the blind-man for me.

PROCULA

Gladly.

ROMULUS

I'm going to lounge around for a while in the shops of the Sacred Way. Down there, at the corner of the street are some very diverting pantomimes, and dancers form Cadiz, sufficiently enticing—and then I was forgetting. It's the hour they are going to drag the cadaver of Plautus to the pillory, and I want to be there to scream: Down with Tiberius.

PROCULA

Your tongue will end by doing you harm.

ROMULUS

Poor Procula, you know nothing about politics.

PROCULA

Indeed, it's true.

ROMULUS

(leaving)

Goodbye, Barbarian.

PROCULA

Goodbye, citizen of Rome.

(to old man)

Come into my shop and you can rest.

(an affirmative gesture by the old man)

Would you give me your hand so I can lead you?

(another nod of the head)

Is he mute, too?

(the old man slowly gives him his hand)

That hand is cold like that of a cadaver!

(The old man goes into the workshop.

BLANDINE

No more hope, Chariclea, I've ruined him.

CHARICLEA

Ah, it's a great misfortune.

BLANDINE

Lost. My cross, my dear cross.

PROCULA

Here it is, Madame.

BLANDINE

Yes, that's it, that's really it. Thanks, Procula, thanks

PROCULA

You know my name?

BLANDINE

Say rather, I haven't forgotten.

PROCULA

You remember me?

BLANDINE

Didn't you share the games of my childhood?

PROCULA

And I, who, each evening, seeing you pass, didn't even dare.

BLANDINE

I couldn't actually speak to you first. Well, here you are, become a man of business, a clever worker, and all the nobility of Rome comes to your place. Chariclea pretended that commercial success had turned your head and that you had become too proud to recognize your friends of yesteryear. Don't you say anything to this naughty nurse who scolded us when others caressed us.

CHARICLEA

Your hand, my dear son.

BLANDINE

And don't you see I'm holding out mine to you?

PROCULA

O radiant past! O all joys, all enchantments. The sturdy villa, the basins in which goldfish played, the granite sphinx, the great bulls of Clytumnus, Spring flowers, golden birds in their flight—

BLANDINE

My mother was living then!

CHARICLEA

And when's the wedding, my son?

PROCULA

What wedding?

CHARICLEA

Yours.

PROCULA

Why, I'm not thinking of it.

BLANDINE

I promise an expensive gift to your fiancée.

PROCULA (aside)

Ah, the awakening. Fall back to earth, slave—the wings of your dream are broken.

BLANDINE

Why this cloud ob your face? Aren't you happy?

PROCULA

Can a slave be happy, Madame? Is there a God for men of misery and servitude?

BLANDINE

Yes, Procula!—Listen, my father was a Questor in Jerusalem. I was barely seven. One night I was on the terrace with my mother and Chariclea. Iin the streets and on the square there was a large and very agitated multitude. I asked my mother what was going on. She pointed to a man with her finger—a condemned man being led to execution. He was covered with a purple cloak and a crown of thorns which was nailed into his flesh. He held a reed in his right hand and bore a heavy cross on his shoulders.

Men, women and children pursued him with insults and mockery, overwhelming him with blows and scratching his face. When he passed before us, he raised his head and cast a glance at us so full of kindness, of sorrow and forgiveness that an invincible force made us fall to our knees, and we remained there for a very long while, faces in our hands. The last glance of the just had saved our souls.

PROCULA

Who was this man, really?

BLANDINE

He was the God of all those who suffered, were they the least of slaves. He will be, I hope, that of Procula.

PROCULA

Yes, since he is yours.

CHARICLEA

Those noises, this crowd.

(aside, looking off)

Ah, it's horrible.

(aloud)

Come, my young mistress, come.

BLANDINE (to Procula)

We will see each other again.

(She leaves with Chariclea. Night has come on completely.)

PROCULA

O Unknown God! All that I ask of you is to be able to die for her!

(Groups of people come on stage. The old man pokes his head out of the shop.

Kiomara comes to him rapidly.)

KIOMARA (low to the old geezer)

Everything is ready!

(An executioner enters by torch light, dragging Plautus's body in a fish-net.)

EXECUTIONER

Make way! Make way! Let pass the justice of Tiberius.

CROWD

No, no.

ROMULUS

Stop a moment. We want to speak to the deceased according to the custom. We want to give him our messages for the other world.

EXECUTIONER

Make way, in the name of Tiberius, make way!

CROWD

Down! Down!

(They beat the Executioner who takes to his heels.)

ROMULUS

Now, citizens of Rome—be silent!

CROWD

Speak! Speak!

ROMULUS

Lord Plautus, I charge you to tell Augustus that the 43 million sesterces, donated by him to the Roman people in his will has not yet been disbursed by Tiberius.

CROWD

It's true! Bravo! Bravo! Long live Augustus! Down with Tiberius.

ROMULUS

Someone else's turn now.

PORCIUS

My turn. —Friend Plautus, tell your ancestor Opimius, whose wine we tasted yesterday evening, that the time of good meals is over, and that we cannot savor in peace dishes prepared by Sicilian chefs—

(Laughter and hoots from the crowd.)

ROMULUS

Don't you recognize the orator? It's Porcius, the drunk; Porcius, the glutton.

CROWD

Down with Porcius!

(They shove him.)

Down! Down!

PORCIUS (aside)

One will never make anything of these ragamuffins.

SENECA

I demand to speak.

CROWD

Silence! Listen! Silence!

SENECA (after having spit and coughed)

I won't tell you O Manes of Senator Plautus, the color of Venus' hair, the day of the birth of Hercules, the number of Achilles' hair—

(Laughter and hoots)

CROWD

Enough! Enough!

SENECA

I won't tell you—

CROWD

Down with the orator!

ROMULUS

It's Seneca, the philosopher, Seneca, the lawyer, Seneca, the merchant of phrases—

CROWD

Down with him! Down with him!

SENECA

In the name of the twelve gread Gods—

ROMULUS

If he doesn't shut up, throw him in the Tiber—

CROWD

Yes, yes.

SENECA

Mercy, my good friends, mercy.

CROWD

In the Tiber! In the Tiber!

NERVA (appearing)

Stop!

ALL

Nerva!

AURELIUS

Yes, citizens! The only man who is worthy of being your leader.

ROMULUS

Silence, now, and let everyone form up.

(To Nerva)

Approach, Lord, come confide to Plautus your message to the land of the shadows.

NERVA

When Tiberius strikes our friends and our neighbors he forbids regrets, he makes a crime of our tears. He orders the mother whose son he kills to put laurels on her door. He orders the son whose father he has killed to kiss his merciful hand; as for me, I declare that I honor the victims of Tiberius, that I approach them without fear, and that I hold them as sacred! Allow me then, O Death, to shake your cold hand. Let me turn your livid face toward the stars. Hear, O Death, my funereal goodbyes! Tell Julius Caesar that under Tiberius, barbarians insult the frontiers of the Empire, and that Rome agonizes in blood. Tell Augustus to send us from the depth of his tomb, a breath of honor and justie, to revive in us the faith of our ancestors, and to make Tiberius quake in his infamous island. Tell the Republicans, those vanquished at Pharsalus, that we have all sworn on your cadaver, eternal hate to tyranny!

ALL

Eternal hate!

ROMULUS

Listen—that marching, that noise of arms!

CROWD (with terror)

The Praetorians!

NERVA

Yes, the Praetorians—who are with us! The Praetorians that Caligula is leading to us!

(The old geezer makes a violent gesture)

KIOMARA (low)

Patience, will you!

(Numerous soldiers invade the square)

CROWD

Long live Caligula! Long live the Praetorians!

CALIGULA

Block all the streets!

(Turning to the Patricians)

In the name of Tiberius, I arrest you!

NERVA

Treason!

CALIGULA

You understand that resistance is useless.

KIOMARA (low to old geezer)

There! You see!

(The Old Geezer strides forward and throws back the hood that hid his face.)

ALL (recognizing him)

Tiberius!

TIBERIUS (to Caligula)

By Hercules! Now there's a fine nephew.

CALIGULA (bending his knee)

Caesar!

TIBERIUS

Hug me, will you, my dear Caius!

(aside)

Someone must have warned him I was in Rome.

(looking at Kiomara)

She, perhaps!

CALIGULA (aside)

Kiomara didn't deceive me.

(aloud)

Caesar, my devotion, my respect.

TIBERIUS

Fine, fine. I know your heart.

NERVA (to Caligula)

Do you deny that this very morning you conspired with us?

PATRICIANS

Yes, yes.

CALIGULA

I feigned to conspire.

TIBERIUS

He feigned, the dear child, and you suspected nothing. He's clever at feigning. —Yes, it's me, it's really me, old Tiberius, that was thought to be at Capri, who comes like this to surprise his good people. Eh, what? Your heart didn't tell you I was in Rome, in your midst.? I've been here for the last two days in this disguise, alone with Kiomara, my faithful Gaul. I haven't wasted my time, I swear to you. I heard everything, saw all, guessed all, and I know better than ever the feelings of the people of Rome for their master. You see me filled with gratitude.

NERVA (aside)

He plays with his prey before tearing it to piees.

AURELIUS

By Jove, I really feel his claws.

TIBERIUS

Alas! Why is there a cloud in my sky? What, my good friends, you conspire against me?

PORCIUS

Mercy, Tiberius, mercy.

(He falls to his knees with Seneca and several others.)

AURELIUS

Wretched cowards!

TIBERIUS

Baseness after treachery. Indeed, they're all the same.

NERVA

Don't insult those whose heads remain unbowed, whose eyes look you in the face!

TIBERIUS

Right! Now there are the traditions of old Rome. I recognize there, indeed, probity, justice, heroic severity—in a word, the Republican Nerva!

(aside)

All my hate for this one!

(aloud)

They say you have a charming daughter—present her to me.

NERVA

You won't tear her from the altar of Vesta.

(Blandine enters with Chariclea.)

BLANDINE

Father!

NERVA

Wretched hild!

TIBERIUS

Charming indeed.

BLANDINE (on her knees to Tiberius)

Caesar, prove that you are master by pardoning—

TIBERIUS

An innocent and sweet girl an disarm the powers of the earth. Well yes, I pardon. I'm doing even more, I'm taking you all to Capri where we will celebrate peace "en famille"—in a magnificent feast. You know, Caesar has this in common with Jupiter, he gets bored, sometimes. I need to distract myself and I cannot find a better opportunity to cheer myself up a little.

ROMULUS

If I could just squirm away—

(A Praetorian pushes him back brutally)

TIBERIUS

Ah, it's you, Citizen of Rome! You accuse me of being miserly with spectacles; I will give you an astonishing one in which you shall have a role as an actor. As for the will of Augustus, we'll talk about it again, and you won't reproach Tiberius for paying his debts. Let's get going. I'm in haste to show this beautiful girl (pointing to Blandine) the marvels of my imperial isle.

CHARICLEA (to Procula)

She's lost.

TIBERIUS

Let's go, my guests.

PROCULA

Don't forget me, Caesar.

TIBERIUS

Who are you?

PROCULA

Their accomplice. Because I was the one who sold them weapons.

TIBERIUS

To Capri!

CURTAIN

ACT II

SCENE II: THE SLAVES

An atrium open to the sky. In perspective, the Villa of Tiberius and the isle of Capri.

KIOMARA

No sail on the horizon as yet. Vainly I await the agreed signal. Gods of terror and shadows, implacable Gods that my ancestors adored, guide to Capri the avengers of Gaul.

CALIGULA

You are alone.

KIOMARA

Alone.

CALIGULA

Ah!

(He looks around him suspiciously)

What are you looking at with so much attention?

KIOMARA

Heaven—earth!

CALIGULA

And that interests you?

KIOMARA

Yes! I interrogate space and space replies to me. We understand each other through mysterious affinities. Everything in nature speaks, the wave that foams, the cloud that flies.

CALIGULA

I thought that prophetesses like you preferred night to day.

KIOMARA

It's true. And when you entered I cursed quietly the tardiness of the Sun, I invoked the return of cold shades so as to read in the stars.

CALIGULA

So they read many things in the stars?

KIOMARA

Everything!

CALIGULA

Truly?

KIOMARA

Haven't they announced to me that Caligula will reign?

CALIGULA

Shut up! Shut up!

KIOMARA

The prediction shocks you to such a degree?

CALIGULA

Reign! Why, I could only do it through the death of Tiberius.

KIOMARA

Well?

CALIGULA (raising his voice)

Tiberius die! The illustrious, the glorious, the divine Tiberius—it would be a most great misfortune for me—just to survive Tiberius. Why that would be horrible.

KIOMARA

It would be natural. Tiberius is old and you are young.

CALIGULA

Heavens, Kiomara, would you like me to tell you the stars lied? I am sure that I will die before Tiberius. There are omens that do not deceive. Yes, I will die young., like all my brothers, I am very weak, I cough till my chest breaks. I have one of those unforgiving maladies.

KIOMARA (with a smile)

Ill—you?

CALIGULA

My pallor proves it sufficiently.

KIOMARA

Indeed, you are quite pale.

(aside)

Does he paint his face, I wonder.

CALIGULA

I've spent a frightful night and I'm going to put myself back to bed because fever is devouring me. Caligula, Empreror—mockery. And what would I make of power, poor little prince that I am? Immortal gods, what will become of the scepter in my hands? I am nothing; I've never been capable of doing anything. I still love to play with children, I am still only a puny embryo, and ill come. Ah, ah, ah, Rome would indeed be well governed and the universe have a fine master!

KIOMARA (aside)

What kind of comedy is he playing?

CALIGULA

Whereas Tiberius was veritably born for the throne! He's got calm, wisdom, authority, genius; he knows the secrets of power to their depths, and he cleverly manipulates the springs. Tiberius deserves to be immortal; what am I saying? He is already! Don't talk to me anymore of your stars—let little Caius die crushed underfoot like an insect—but let Tiberius live eternally.

KIOMARA

Marvelous! How can he hear you?

CALIGULA

Ah, he doesn't know how much I love him and venerate him. He's unaware of all the gratitude I have for his sovereign kindnesses. There are evil folks who seek to ruin me in his mind—to persuade him that I am repaying him with ingratitude, and that I am criminal enough to conspire—

KIOMARA

Tiberius doesn't believe them.

CALIGULA

Assuredly, because he is justice itself. Nonetheless, these slanders—I've noticed them with profound sorrow, render his looks more suspicious, more severe. Thus, since he has returned from Rome with his captives, he hasn't even said a word to me; he is plotting by himself some terrible vengeance, and I know nothing about this mysterious fest that he intends to give Nerva and all the other plotters. Oh, I swear to you, the day in which I shall have lost the good graces of my master will be the last day of my life. I won't wait for the Fates to finish me off, I will kill myself from despair.

(He throws himself at the feet of Tiberius who raises him up.)

KIOMARA

Ah. I understand everything. The young tiger sniffed the old one.

CALIGULA (prostrated)

My benefactor! My father!

TIBERIUS

Enough tenderness, Caius, enough.

(He dismisses Caligula with a gesture.)

CALIGULA

Ah, how wretched I am!

(He weeps.)

TIBERIUS (aside)

Real tears!

CALIGULA (aside)

I have to think seriously about saving my head.

(He bows and leaves.)

TIBERIUS

That child is really tough!

KIOMARA

He's worthy of reigning.

TIBERIUS

You like him.

KIOMARA

After you.

TIBERIUS

Understood. Let him wait then, and be careful not to conspire. I don't like heirs who are too impatient.

KIOMARA

When did Caius conspire?

TIBERIUS

You know better than anyone.

KIOMARA

Me?

TIBERIUS

Listen, Gallic lady. I don't confound you in the vulgar rabble of slaves. You possess the art of spelling out those characters traced on the book of the heavens by the shivering luminescence of lightning bolts. Thrasyllus, my astrologer is less capable than you in nocturnal incantations, and there's not a Thracian witch that gathers with greater certitude venomous herbs in the dark mosses where serpents glide; thus I reward your science; I do it justice, and I've consulted it sometimes without believing it too much. Still, I advice you, don't abuse my indulgent kindness, and be careful never to deceive me—because I will break you pitilessly.

KIOMARA

I have less fear of death than those who give it.

TIBERIUS

What are you saying between your teeth?

KIOMARA

Isay that I know my honor as I know that of others.

TIBERIUS (gently)

Look, understand me carefully. I'm not hostile to you—but I have the right to reproach you. Thus, the evening of the revolt you left me on the square before the palace of Nerva, on the pretext of bringing the Praetorians to my assistance, but in reality it was to warn Caligula who was certainly part of the conspiracy—of my presence. For him to conspire against me, him, this earthworm—Oh, I will remember.

KIOMARA

Rather forget. Youth is subject to error, but returns quickly to good. Didn't you hear him just now profess his love and admiration for you? And surely he couldn't have suspected you were there.

TIBERIUS

I'm not so sure of that.

KIOMARA

In the end, what do you want? Someday, will you, nil you, Tiberius must die. You need a successor.

TIBERIUS

An heir, right?

KIOMARA

Naturally.

TIBERIUS

Oh, an heir who has the strength, beauty, youth, when you are ugly, bald and decrepit, an insolent heir that the cowardly multitude adores and celebrates in your place; a rapacious and ingrate heir who sleeps in your bed, counts your money, empties your wine ellars, and steals your mistresses. Ah, these thoughts render me furious, and that's why I hate Caligula so much!

KIOMARA

You are wrong. Let him reign after you—isn't he better than any other for the happiness of the Roman people?

TIBERIUS

Yes, you are right. For the happiness of the Roman people. —But let's speak of something else. Did you punctually execute my orders?

KIOMARA

It was easy.

TIBERIUS

You wrote all the names of my slaves and you put them in an urn?

KIOMARA

Here it is.

TIBERIUS

Without forgetting one.

KIOMARA

Not even Borgatas the blind.

TIBERIUS

And where are they now.

KIOMARA (pointing to a door)

They are waiting there. In accordance with your desires, I made them drink a profusion of the most heady wine.

TIBERIUS

And Nerva's daughter?

KIOMARA (pointing to another door)

She's here.

TIBERIUS

Make her come.

KIOMARA

Enter, maiden.

BLANDINE (entering)

Caesar.

TIBERIUS

Don't tremble so. No one wants to harm you.

BLANDINE

Why then have they separated me from my father?

TIBERIUS

Aren't you near me?

BLANDINE

I am in Capri.

TIBERIUS

Is that name so frightening?

BLANDINE (shivering)

Oh!

TIBERIUS

Come on. I see that in your strict Patrician families they quickly instruct young girls and make them learn—in code words, it's agreed, the secrets of the cursed island where Tiberius shuts himself up. That way there are a thousand tales of timid virgins who are carried away from their hearths to become the prey of a monster. Oh, I know these proud ones well, and I've learned to read in their chaste hearts. They lower their eyes and veil their faces—they are shocked in advance at the embraces of Caesar. But there's not one of them who's not ambitious at bottom for the title of "sovereign's favorite."

BLANDINE

For the daughter of Nerva that would be the height of shame and horror.

TIBERIUS

So be it! You're an exception—I really hope so. But it's not a question of you. Indeed, Tiberius is not worthy of aspiring to so many charms. Also, all sighing with respect, he will allow that happiness to those younger than he.

BLANDINE

My God!

TIBERIUS

Do you know, Blandine, that your beauty is making cruel ravages in Capri?

BLANDINE

I don't understand anything of your words, But they have a hidden sense which shocks and freezes me.

TIBERIUS

You have lovers from all nations.

BLANDINE (with a scream)

Where is my father?

TIBERIUS

You won't see him until you are married.

BLANDINE

Married!

TIBERIUS

Yes, I am going to give you a spouse from my house—Goodness, I don't know yet if he'll be Parthian, African, Cambrian, or a Gaul. I told you that the whole universe adores you.

(Blandine looks him in the face and rises in proud modesty.)

BLANDINE

They are mistaken when they say you are clever in dissembling. A ferocious hates bursts out of your eyes despite you. Hate of that which is noble, courageous and without stain, hate of pure families' descent, hate of Roman virtue. So go ahead, avenge yourself. I won't abase myself further in the role of supplicant.

TIBERIUS

You take after your father.

BLANDINE

Thanks to heaven which protects me against you.

TIBERIUS (aside)

Let's see how far this piety, this courage will go, and if Rome has produced another Lucretia.

(Low to Kiomara)

Finish up, I'll be here.

(He leaves the way he came.)

BLANDINE

A woman. Ah, I am saved. You will have pity on me, won't you? Just now, in front of him you didn't dare to take up my defense, and I understand that because this man is living terror, but now that his glance no longer weighs on you, oh, you will come to my aid.

KIOMARA

Shut up, will you!

BLANDINE

No, no. I press your hands, I embrace your clothes. I kept my head high before Tiberius, but it's no shame for one woman to implore another. Save me! Save me!

KIOMARA

You are mad!

BLANDINE

You reject me?

KIOMARA

Look on the iron ring riveted to my arm. I have a master, I must obey.

BLANDINE

Why, in that case, I am lost.

KIOMARA

I believe it.

BLANDINE

Lost. Oh, no, it's impossible! You won't be an accomplice to this infamy.

KIOMARA

Hey! What's the honor of a Patrician woman of Rome to me? Is that my concern? So much the better if they suffer—because I've suffered in front of them, so much the better if they roll in the filth and mud where I am still struggling, still soiled and degraded myself. I enjoy their abasement, their ignominy, and these hands of mine are happy to cast one more sacrifice into the abyss, it's the only joy still permitted to me.

BLANDINE

Mercy! Pity in the name of your father, ah, of your mother.

KIOMARA

My mother! She was executed for escaping from servitude,—my father, your soldiers butchered him. As for me, they tore me from an altar, they struck me in a cowardly way, they degraded me in blood by the hair, and finally they sold me, still a child to a courtesan from Capri who destined me for the ogre of Tiberius.

BLANDINE

Ah, this is horrible. But I am not for nothing in your misfortune.

KIOMARA

What do you know about it? Wasn't Nerva one of the executioners of Gaul?

Don't waste your effort trying to soften me, and expect no pity from me. Perhaps you've been told of Kiomara a Gallic slave who has commerce with demons and the dead, who nourishes the furors of Tiberius, and prepares his terrible poisons. Kiomara, that's me.

BLANDINE

Powerful Gods!

KIOMARA

Tiberius and me, we understand each other, and I serve him well—only he hates Rome more than I do. And he is all powerful to do evil. A woman, you were saying just now. I am not a woman. I am vengeance.

(An explosion of noisy voices outside)

CHORUS OF SLAVES

Tiberius is partying in Capri,

And drags us to the prey.

Let's sing!

Tiberius is good to his slaves.

And breaks for a moment no bonds.

Let's drink.

BLANDINE

What are those threatening voices?

KIOMARA

The slaves of Tiberius are happy today.

CHORUS OF SLAVES

This evening, tumult, orgy.

And forget the powerful yoke

Tomorrow death! So be it without liberty—

Man doesn't cling to life.

KIOMARA

There is a whole legion of nameless savages, without family, without country, ignoble cargo brought from the North, and from the hold in the entrails of the ship, sold in the markets of Rome. Captives, conquered, renegades, deserters, adept in all baseness, brutalized by servitude, and who, for the most part, have northing human about them. Not ev3en the face. Well, to their ferocity, Tiberius has once again added that of wine.

BLANDINE

O horror!

KIOMARA

Hold on, I'm going to repeat their word to you.

(She repeats the chorus.)

Today from the ancient amphora, the wine streams in golden waves. And the kisses most savory still

Of the young Patrician.

Do you understand, Blandine

"And the most savory kisses,

Of the young Patrician."?

BLANDINE

Oh, it's a monstrous illusion, right? Nothing more. All this is not real. A breath will suffice to dissipate these shadows, to make these hideous ghosts vanish. They only want to frighten me, I am sure. Tiberius won't trample under his feet the laws he has respected, despite his crimes—the most sacred laws of my country.

KIOMARA

Laws—in Capri?

BLANDINE

I repeat to you that even here, all Rome protects me, and that it surrounds me like an impenetrable sanctuary.

KIOMARA

Why, they cannot have told you how the daughter of Sejanus died.

BLANDINE

No.

KIOMARA

She was a poor child, white like a dove, frail like a reed, weeping without understanding why she was being seized, and asking with adorable grace what wrong she had done. Surely, the laws protected her also, and there was no example of a virgin being put to death. What expedient seized Tiberius who respects the laws? Before killing her he had the executioner dishonor her.

BLANDINE

Infamy!

KIOMARA

Don't pity yourself. You've got a much better share than she did, you have slaves for suitors.

(Raising her voice.)

Come in, the rest of you.

(Enter Brogatar, Alben, Naiser, then Procula.)

KIOMARA

Here's the fiancée that Tiberius gives you.

ALL

Long live Tiberius!

(Blandine wraps herself in her veil and clasps it tight with both hands.)

NARSES

We cannot see her.

ALBIN

Down with the veil.

BROGATAR

I'll smash the first one who disputes her with me.

KIOMARA

Silence, Brogatar. And wait until the decree is pronounced.

BROGATAR

No, I don't wish—

KIOMARA

It's the master's order.

BROGATAR

Then hurry up.

BLANDINE

Leave me alone, leave me alone.

NARSES

This is amusing.

ALBIN

One would say a fawn caught in a net.

BLANDINE

Help! Help!

BROGATAR

Quiet down. You are caught.

KIOMARA (pointing to the urn)

All your names are in there.

NARSES

You haven't forgotten anyone, at least?

KIOMARA

No one.

PROCULA

And what about me?

BLANDINE

Procula!

(She runs to him.)

Ah, you are coming to my aid!

PROCULA (coldly)

I'm coming to join my name to that of the others.

BLANDINE

What are you saying?

PROCULA

I am saying that I would really like to win.

BLANDINE

Oh!

BROGATAR (to Procular)

Who are you?

PROCULA

Get back, friend, I don't like to be spoken to so close.

BROGATAR

You'll get used to it.

PROCULA

You must pass for very strong, but the lion doesn't fear the bull.

(He pushes him back)

BROGATAR

By Hell!

KIOMARA (separating them)

Enough!

(aside, observing Procula)

That look—those features!—Chimera! Death doesn't give up its prey.

PROCULA

Come on, woman, write my name and cast it in the urn with the others.

KIOMARA

No.

PROCULA

Why?

KIOMARA

You don't belong to Tiberius.

PROCULA

I am a slave, too. Who cares who the master is? There's a noble girl to be won at random, and I want to be a part of it.

KIOMARA

That's impossible.

PROCULA

Then into the sea with all this.

(He grabs the urn and hurls it out the window.)

ALL

Vengeance.

TIBERIUS (entering)

Who is so bold as to oppose the will of Tiberius?

(To Procula)

Ah, I recognize you—you admitted you were part of the conspiracy.

PROCULA

I lied, Caesar.

TIBERIUS

Why did you denounce yourself?

PROCULA

Because you would have taken away this young girl, and I didn't want to leave her.

TIBERIUS

Through devotion, no question.

(On these words Blandine opens her veil and raises her eyes with hope to Procula, who remains motionless.)

You are one of those model slaves who sacrifice themselves at need to save their master.

PROCULA

No, Caesar, Im am not one of those ninnies, far from having affection and gratitude for the one I serve, I would be happy to do him ill.

TIBERIUS

You hate Nerva?

PROCULA

More than anybody.

(Blandine falls back crushed.)

TIBERIUS

Still, he was good to you.

PROCULA

Is a master ever good?

TIBERIUS

You are seeking to deceive me. I am sure you followed Blandine from devotion.

PROCULA

No, but from love.

TIBERIUS

Ah—

PROCULA

I followed her to protect her—not because she's the master's daughter, but because I love her passionately, and I don't want her to belong to anyone else.

I love her to such a degree that if you had wanted to take her I would have fought against you even to torture, even to death.

TIBERIUS

Truly?

PORCIUS

Imagine an immense, unconquerable savage passion, a passion long contained like a crime in the folds of the heart, in senseless tears, in hopeless desires, which bursts out suddenly with the violence of a tempest, a love, that's still like vengeance. Once at Capri, I knew you would give Blandine up to your slaves, so I seized the opportunity to get to her—the only opportunity, perhaps, I'd ever get, and I came to demand my place.

TIBERIUS

Ah, that's the way it is. Well, since by throwing the uirn into the sea you've made the decree of destiny impossible, I'll substitute my sovereign will for it.

(A long silence.)

Weighing everything

(To Brogatas)

It's to you I give her.

PORCIUS (leaping in front of her)

Let him come to get her.

BROGATAR

Caesar?

TIBERIUS

I authorize you.

BLANDINE

Oh, I have no more strength or courage.

BROGATAR (to Procula)

The two of us!

PORCIUS

Don't come near!

BROGATAR

This girl belongs to me.

(He rushes Procula who arms himself with a dagger and strikes him)

PORCIUS

In that case, die.

(Brogatas falls, Blandine utters a scream and faints in Procula's arms.)

TIBERIUS

Well killed.

PORCIUS

What do you say to that, Tiberius? Have I given evidence? The slave assassin, is he worthy of the daughter of Nerva?

TIBERIUS

Keep her, indeed! The proud Roman will be happy to have such a son-in-law. Open the nuptial chamber to the happy couple

PORCIUS

At last! I've succeeded!

TIBERIUS

Vulture with bloody talons, carry off your prey.

(Procula leads the quaking Blandine away.)

KIOMARA (looking outside)

The signal. Ah, here are the avengers.

TIBERIUS

To the others now. The party's beginning well!

CURTAIN

SCENE III: A FEAST IN CAPRI

A magnificent festive hall.

TIBERIUS

Come, my dear guests, come! Drink, eat, enjoy yourselves at my expense. This is how Tiberius takes vengeance.

PORCIUS

It's unheard of, it's marvel.ous, it's Olympian. In memory of this fest tomorrow I will sacrifice a goose to Jupiter.

E*

Porcius is drunk like a street porter.

PORCIUS

O Divine Caesar. The blindfold is falling from my eyes, and I declare that in conspiring against you we were all great rogues.

AURELIUS

Speak for yourself, old madcap.

PORCIUS

And that fool of an Aurelius who told us to beware Caesar's feasts.

TIBERIUS

They are always slandering me.

PORCIUS

I would like to be metamorphised into a fountain if the roasts I am attacking here is not a present of Colchos.

TIBERIUS

Ah, you are a connoisseur.

PORCIUS

I've made studies so deep that I am never deceived. Thus, Cos produced this wine; Phasus these birds; Africa these shell fish. These snails were raised on an island quite sheltered from the Sun. As for these oysters they came from Britain, but they've been fattened and refreshed in a park near Lucrin—that's what makes them so delicious.

TIBERIUS

Admirable. A final question, Porcius—what is the prodigy of dishes?

PORCIUS

A plate of nightingale tongues.

TIBERIUS

Let Porcius be served one.

PORCIUS

Long live Tiberius, the great, the inimitable, the divine Tiberius! O the beautiful goose that tomorrow I shall sacrifice to the master of the gods.

TIBERIUS

Right. You clearly understand the destiny of man down here.

PORCIUS

It's to have the best meals one can.

TIBERIUS

Come on, my guests, imitate Porcius. Some appetite, some verve, and far from us lugubrious cases to hear the prattlers of the Forum. Tiberius is an old miser who wears a patched tunic, drinks cheap wine, and eats at his meals only boiled game, and for economy sends his fishes to be sold in the markets. Admit that he doesn't do things badly when he sets his mind to it, and we are not yet at the first service. Surprises are reserved for you.

AURELIUS

Indeed, I hope so!

(low to Natalis)

I suppose that you don't trust in his clemency?

NATALIS

Didn't Augustus say as he was dying, "I pity the Roman people; they're going to be crushed under very slow chewing."

AURELIUS

It's the same. He's only carefully digesting his victims with slow sensuality. Don't be sad, will you! It's very curious to observe the meals of the monster.

TIBERIUS (to Romulus)

You aren't eating?

ROMULUS

Caesar is very good. I'm not hungry.

TIBERIUS

You aren't drinking either.

ROMULUS

Caesar is indeed good, I'm not thirsty.

TIBERIUS

What are you thinking about?

ROMULUS

I'm thinking of Rome, Caesar, of the obelisk, of the Arch of Triumph, of my sauntering on the hill of gardens to go see the Rhinoceros and the Giraffe!

TIBERIUS

You love it a lot, your Rome?

ROMULUS

Yes, I love it. But for the rest of us, there's no life, no Sun, except there.

TIBERIUS

Yes, the Rome of Augustus, right? The city that, in his words, he received in bricks and left in marble. The city of noise, dust and turbulent multitudes. To each his own tastes. I prefer Capri. But ob the subject of Augustus, I am your debtor, citizen Romulus.

ROMULUS

Oh, I'm not clamoring for anything.

TIBERIUS

You would be wrong, since it is your right. You will be paid, my friend, completely paid.

ROMULUS (aside)

I no longer have a drop of blood in my veins.

TIBERIUS

Let the part revive with more vigor and dazzle. And, since no party is complete without poetry, without music, take up your harps, young Rhodians. Kiomara will recite to us the verses of Afranius.

KIOMARA (declaiming)

Patricians, Tiberius fests you at his feasts,

Laurel and rose are entwined with song

Make a necklace of beautiful lovers arms

Hurry to enjoy,—death is over your heads

Be drunken to forget!

Applaud he who dies well, hiss the one who dies without grace.

The public is rushing quickly to other battles,

Let them return to return to rake the blushing sand

And let a thousand perfumes spread through space,

Correcting the acrid odor of blood!

Drink, laugh, sing! Ours, ancient masterpieces,

Obelisks of the Niles, marbles from the Parthenon,

Jasper, emeralds, onyx—ours, luxury without name.

Gigantic pleasures, frenetic debauches,

No one brings their riches to Pluto.

Ephesus is consecrated to proud Diana.

Minerva dwells in Athens, Jupitor Stator

Was sculpted by Phidias in ivory and gold

Pluto reigns in hell, but the God of Capri,

Tiberius is greater still than he.

AURELIUS

Bravo, slave. There are images in these verses which completely depict the Roman Patrician. Yes, this world is a circus, and we are gladiators. The great thing for us. The only thing, must be to smile at the final hour, and not end clumsily Bravo, I tell you. So by the three Fates, I Aurelius, an old man of thirty, whose worn out stomach barely supports water, I intend, in the honor of poesy, to empty a cup of wine from Cyprus. I drink to death!

(A Patrician near him raises his cup at the same time.

PATRICIAN

To death!

AURELIUS

I know a man here who isn't drinking this toast.

TIBERIUS

Who's that?

AURELIUS

You!

TIBERIUS

You are mistaken.

(drinking)

To death

(aside)

Of my enemies.

(aloud)

I'm not as enthusiastic about your verses. There's one that is especially absurd.

The last that calls me God. Ah, if I were a god, I'd be richer than I am—also!

AURELIUS (to Evander)

Do you see it coming? He's going to make us pay for the cook and the orchestra.

TIBERIUS

You are uneasy, perhaps, that my affairs aren't going well. Still, that's the exact truth. First of all, I've spent mad sums for this feast.

AURELIUS (low to Evander)

Here we go!

TIBERIUS

For certain. I don't regret it because with one's friends one mustn't consider expenses; what affects me deeply, is not yet to have enough to execute the Will of Augustus, a debt so legitimate and sacred, as Romulus has so strongly put it.

ROMULUS

I swear to you, Caesar, I demand nothing more.

TIBERIUS

If I'm slow, my child, it's not bad will, but real indigence.

ROMULUS

I believe it, Caesar, I believe it, and I renounce the inheritance.

TIBERIUS

Generous citizen! This abnegation touches me, but I don't accept it. May Augustus forgive me if, to procure the necessary money, I have recourse to cruel expedients! Narses, go bring the coffer of relics. You know the veneration I've always had for Augustus living, and what a deep cult I've dedicated to his memory. Why, all that's contained in this coffer comes from him. Judge what it costs me to separate myself from these precious remains! Finally, I hold back my tears, I impose silence on my sorrow, since the interest of the Roman people forces such a sacrifice on me. Ah, at least, in the moment in which I resigned myself to sacrificing these sacred objects to find money, I am happy to have you for purchasers, to see these treasures pass into your noble hands, which, for the love of Augustus, you are going to fight over with a filial animosity. Silence, now, silence! The sale is going to begin and I myself, will fill the office of auctioneer. I have no need to tell you that the more dearly you pay, the more respect you manifest for Augustus. Consequently, the more you have the right to my good graces! An augural baton a hundred thousand sesterces, one hundred twenty then, and one hundred fifty thousand. Two hundred thousand. And then? Come on, I'm waiting. This baton is priceless. Think that it was handled by Augustus. One hundred fifty thousand more—that's fine. You've put something on the side. Fifty thousand more, I believe. Four hundred thousand sesterces. Watch out, I'm going to say "sold". They add two hundred thousand over here. Two hundred thousand over there with the one hundred thousand

Of Coronius, that makes a million and I say "sold." Lucky man, it's a gift. Next—

A ceremo0nial cloak—Augustus wore it fifty years ago the day he triumphed over the Germans. Purple, a bit threadbare, but authentically historic. Five million sesterces, six, seven, eight, nine, ten million sesterces. It's yours. You can boast of having made a great bargain. Finally auctioned! The object most simple in appearance, but without contradiction the most precious of all—wjhich reveals the domestic manners of the great man: a pair of sandals from Augustus's bedroom. Five million sesterces. What's it mean? You are silent. Six million. Go on, misers that you are. Aren't you ashamed to be so slow? Which of you adds three million without hesitating? Porcius, mighty fine! Think that Augustus is looking at you. A little courage! It's to pay what he owes these honest citizens of Rome. The sandals for ten million to Porcius! Now there's an amateur who doesn't hesitate, he just keeps going.

NARSES

Why, Lord, I think he's sleeping.

TIBERIUS

Not at all, not at all. Observe the motion of his head—he makes a sign that he accepts. Oh, I know him! To possess the sandals of Augustus, he doesn't blanche at any sacrifice, he would give twenty millions,—wouldn't you, Porcius? I was sure of it! You see he's giving them! He's still nodding. I intend to favor him for his paiun, and I say "sold" for thirty million sesterces. Pass them to him.

(They rap him on the shoulder and he wakes up.)

PORCIUS

What is it?

TIBERIUS

The sandals of Augustus that you just purchased cheap for thirty million sesterces.

PORCIUS

Just Gods! Why, I was sleeping.

TIBERIUS

What, wretch? You boast of having slept before Caesar?

PORCIUS

The good cheer, the wine—mercy!

TIBERIUS

Yes, I pardon you. So when will you pay up?

PORCIUS

How much do I owe?

TIBERIUS

I told you—thirty million.

PORCIUS

Mercy. But my entire fortune doesn't come to half that.

TIBERIUS

Then you deceived me.

PORCIUS

I was sleeping.

TIBERIUS

You stole from me.

TIBERIUS

In the first place, Im seizing all you possess in payment

PORCIUS

Caesar—

TIBERIUS

After that, as punishment, I condemn you to row in one of my galleys until Pluto takes away your old carcass.

PORCIUS

Pity! Pity!

TIBERIUS

Kick him out the door and let him sleep off his wine.

(The slaves drag out Porcius with hoots.)

AURELIUS (aside)

So much for one.

(aloud)

Is it my turn soon?

TIBERIUS

I reserve for you the most terrible of punishments. I condemn you to live.

AURELIUS

Huh? But I don't want to live, I'm very weary of it.

NATALIS

Friend Aurelius, receive our compliments.

AURELIUS

Tiberius would spare me. Ah, that would be too much misfortune to enjoy. I would be exposed to living to forty. Ah, no indeed, that cannot be, that shall not be.

(low to Patricians)

Would you bet, the rest of you, that I have only a quarter of an hour to live?

NATALIS

What are you going to do?

AURELIUS

Watch—but before all, let's shake hands one last time.

(Meanwhile, Tiberius has whispered to Narses and Kiomara who each leave in different directions.)

TIBERIUS (to Aurelius)

Ingrate, you don't even thank me.

AURELIUS

I will do more, Caesar! I intend to prove all my gratitude to you who give me life like a second father. Madman that I was to disdain it, to curse it, when it has so many intoxications for me—so many delights! I have a villa in Tivoli near Rome, another near Naples for the sea breezes, another in the Appenines for the charm of solitude. I possess as many good lands in Sicily, some claims on the Provinces, shops to let in Rome, and I wanted to die.

TIBERIUS (aside)

He's as rich as that?

AURELIUS

Moreover, in Dalmatia, I have gold mines where they gather fifty pounds of the precious metal daily—and I wanted to die! Isn't it just that after me, all these treasures will pass from my hands to those of the generous man who has returned them to me, and made me feel their worth. Caesar, deign to accept my inheritance.

TIBERIUS

Me? But?

AURELIUS

I want to hasten top take my precautions, because, worn out by debauchery I might die suddenly, as if struck by lightning.

TIBERIUS (aside)

Ah!

AURELIUS

It's more than likely that will be my end. So don't let me lose a moment.

(writing on tablets)

All of you be my witnesses that I constitute Caesar my sole heir.

(Giving the writings to Tiberius.)

Here's a will in six words. Perfectly incontestable.

TIBERIUS

You insist that?

AURELIUS

I beg you.

TIBERIUS

In that case, I accept—in the interest of the people of Rome. Friend Aurelius, this action repurchases many sins, and I want us to drink to concord together.

AURELIUS (with irony)

O magnanimous heart!

TIBERIUS (to a slave)

Daphne, fill the cup of Lord Aurelius from the silver Amphora.

(to Aurelius)

It's my best wine.

AURELIUS

Empty it to the depths.

(after having drunk)

Thanks, Tiberius.

(He sits and his head falls on the table.)

NATALIS

Aurelius—friend—get up, speak to us.

TIBERIUS

Leave him alone, will you! He's doing like Porcius, he's sleeping.

NATALIS

He's dead!

TIBERIUS

Come on, will you!

NATALIS

He's dead.

TIBERIUS

Poor Aurelius. He actually predicted that he would end this way—what do you want. It was a worn out body. Carry him away, the rest of you. In my capacity as heir I will see to his funeral—suitable. I won't send him to the gibbet.

NATALIS

Murderer! Be cursed!

ALL

Be cursed!

TIBERIUS (shrugging)

Always big words, gestures.

ROMULUS

If he could forget me.

TIBERIUS

For the two of us now.

ROMULUS (aside)

Oof!

TIBERIUS

After exact calculations, as an individual fraction of the Roman people, you receive for your share of the Will of Augustus two bronze asses. I will pay my other creditors later. As you demanded it, I will pay you immediately. It's more just. You see, bawler, that it wasn't worth the trouble to make so much of a fuss for such a small thing.

ROMULUS

Ah, it's true, quite true.

TIBERIUS

On that subject, you charged Plautus to tell Augustus that I didn't pay his debt.

Well, you will do better to run the errand yourself.

ROMULUS

Myself?

TIBERIUS

Eh, yes. I am going to send you to the next world.

ROMULUS

Pity, Caesar!

TIBERIUS

Don't abuse your dignity as a Roman Citizen by begging. I still remember that I

Promised you a role in the spectacle and I intend to keep my word. You are a habitué of the circus, you loved to see blood spilled by combatants and the claws of ferocious beasts dug into naked flesh. Well, you are going to fight lions in the amphitheatre in your turn.

ROMULUS

Me? Me?

TIBERIUS

Let him be metamorphised into a gladiator.

ROMULUS

No, no! Mercy, mercy!

(They drag him to one side, Nerva enters from another.)

TIBERIUS (going to him)

Nerva, why here you are at last. They want you.

NERVA

My daughter, Tiberius! Where is my daughter? Ah, perhaps you've killed her.

TIBERIUS

As if I were the executioner of women.

NERVA

Then return her to me.

TIBERIUS

Be patient a bit. You are going to see her again.

NERVA

See her again.

TIBERIUS

Don't rejoice too quickly, because if your daughter is living, there's someone dead in your house.

NERVA

Who?

TIBERIUS

Your honor! Yes, it's a pleasant adventure. Imagine that in arriving in Capri, Blandine was smitten with a handsome man who remained with her all n ight.

NERVA

Vengeful Gods!

TIBERIUS

It's true, you will be free of it by marrying them. The most curious thing—your future son-in-law is a slave. He even belongs to you and is named Procula.

NERVA

Him! He who I saved, that I loved, that I thought a noble heart.

TIBERIUS

The generous man is always caught in the same trap! Ingratitude.

NERVA

Ah, executioner! It would have been better to kill her.

TIBERIUS (aside)

I was well aware of that.

(aloud, pointing to Blandine who enters)

You can press her to your breast now.

BLANDINE

Father!

NERVA

Dishonored!

PROCULA

Tiberius lied. She is pure. I deceived you, Caesar, and you are less clever than I thought at reading the thought in one's eyes. The audacious barbarian who roared yesterday has suddenly changed his love into respect, and far from you—he became for her what he's always been, the most humble of servants. His lips which prayed very quietly have not even brushed her chaste hand confided to his care.

TIBERIUS

Now there's a very sublime trait—for a slave!

NERVA

Don't give him that name any more, Tiberius, because I set him free. And I take his hand as my equal.

(To Procula)

The secret of your birth that I've hidden from you until now—would you like to hear it at last?

PROCULA

Oh. Speak, speak.

NERVA

You are of the Gallic race. You descend from the kings of Aquitaine who fought against Rome with so much heroism. You name is not Procula, your name is Vindex!

KIOMARA (aside)

It's him, him!

VINDEX

Ah, so I've actually got a fatherland!

TIBERIUS

Let this Gaul be arrested—it is important for the safety of Rome that the last of these implacable enemies be exterminated.

VINDEX

You will see, my ancestors, if I know how to defy the executioners of Tiberius.

KIOMARA (aside)

Oh! How to save him!

TIBERIUS

As for Blandine that this honest guardian has rendered pure, I'm taking her for myself.

(Nerva seizes a knife from the table, but some slaves snatch it from him.)

Let Lord Nerva do it. He's a reminder of ancient Rome. Virginiua stabbed his daughter. I have that group in all the corners of my palace. The seducer, Appius, is precisely one of my ancestors.

NERVA

Strike her! her! my only daughter—strike her with my hand! No, no, it's impossible. And yet, my daughter, infamy is there which soils you with its look, which calculates its leap like a tiger. Blandine, if your old father has not the courage of Virginius, will you have that of Lucretia?

(Blandine takes the knife and hurls it away.)

What are you doing?

BLANDINE

No suicide!

(pointing to heaven)

Martyrdom!

TIBERIUS

Take her away.

NERVA

Wretches!

BLANDINE

Father, I have nothing to fear; however criminal Tiberius may be, there is one deed I defy him to commit.

TIBERIUS (curious)

What's that?

BLANDINE

That of taking for a mistress a girl guilty of public sacrilege.

TIBERIUS

What are you talking about?

BLANDINE

I'm saying that the Gods of Rome are infamous, that I scorn them, that I insult them! Vile gods, ridiculous or ferocious; Gods of perjury, of prostitution, of carnage, who guive to their adorers the example of all baseness, of all vices, of all crimes!

NERVA

Ah, wretched girl!

BLANDINE

May lightning destroy them and dispose the debris in the mud. The God that I confess came into the world on a cold night, art the hour when the pagan universe celebrated debauchery in purple and gold. But I said that I insult your gods.

(overturning a ststue)

And I prove it.

ALL

Death to the sacrilegious girl, death to the impious one.

BLANDINE (to Tiberius)

So take me now.

ALL

Death! Death!

TIBERIUS

Tiberius, more than anyone, respects the protective Gods of Rome. They chose him for their avenger, and order him to deliver this girl to the lions of the amphitheatre!

ALL

Long live Tiberius! Glory to Tiberius!

BLANDINE

The Circus, torture, the teeth of ferocious beasts, indeed, that's our future. Let the prophesies be accomplished then. Blood pours out in strams, the body falls in shred, but the immortal soul returns to the Creator.

(to Nerva)

Don't weep. This is the day of triumph. Come, borrow faith from my last look.

(to Vindex)

We will see each other on high!

(to Tiberius)

I will pray for you.

ALL

To the lions! To the lions!

VINDEX

Ah, not to be able to defend her!

KIOMARA (low to Vindex)

Hope!

ALL:

To the lions! To the lions!

(They drag away Blandine in the midst of threats and shouts of death.)

CURTAIN

ACT III

SCENE IV: LIONS AND GLADIATORS

A part of the Circus near the tribunal of the Emperor and the great Vestal. The seats are full of spectators. Guards cross the arena with Blandine, and lead her before Tiberius.

TIBERIUS

On your knees proud woman, and demand mercy!

BLANDINE

Never!

TIBERIUS

I order you for the last time to bow your head before Caesar.

BLANDINE

I only bow before my God!

TIBERIUS

Die then, impious one.

(Murmurs and threats.)

TIBERIUS

You are witnesses that we've pushed our imperial clemency to the limits.

ALL

Yes, yes! Death to the Christian. Death!

BLANDINE

I am ready!

ALL

Death! Death!

TIBERIUS

One moment. I want to stay in my duty until the end.

(To Blandine)

Your god had no need to be born expressly to teach the world that it must return good for evil. Tiberius has never practiced any other maxim, and he proves it yet again, by persisting, despite your bravado and outrafges, to give you a valorous champion to defend you. Here he is!

(Romulus is led in, grotesquely dressed in a helmet with a military belt and gladiator's shield. He is greeted with laughter and hoots.)

And this champion is a citizen of Rome.

NARSES (prodding Romulus)

Why move more quickly, will you!

ROMULUS

I have no legs. I have nothing. I casn't see, I can't hear.

NARSES

Come forward.

ROMULUS

Then carry me.

(Romulus is pushed to the foot of the Imperial Throne.)

NARSES

Now, salute Caesar.

ROMULUS

Oh, I really want to.

NARSES

And speak to him.

ROMULUS

What must I say to him?

NARSES

The holy phrase: We who are about to die, salute you.

ROMULUS

Who's going to die?

NARSES

You.

ROMULUS

What do you mean, me?

NARSES

That's what you're here for.

ROMULUS

But I don't want to, you hear. Ah, no indeed, I don't want to.

NARSES

Take this sword.

ROMULUS

What to do?

NARSES

To fight the lions.

(Roaring can be heard off.)

ROMULUS

Those beasts? Never. I don't know how. I've never been trained.

TIBERIUS

Leave him, Narses.

NARSES

But, Lord, he cannot stand on his legs.

TIBERIUS

Obey!

(Romulus falls flat on his face like a block.)

And let the lions be released.

(Narses moves away with the guards.)

ROMULUS

It seems to me I am already in Pluto's domain. Yes, there's old Cerberus. He growls, he shows his teeth. Good evening, good Cerberus, nice Cerberus—brave friend.

(More roaring, he half stands)

TIBERIUS

Look—there he is on his feet. I was sure that the sight of lions would return all his courage to the Citizen of Rome.

ROMULUS

It gives me back my legs.

(He leaves running in the midst of laughter—at which Tiberius gives the signal.)

TIBERIUS

Gladiators—Romulus' place is for whoever wants to take it.

(A gladiator, sword in hand, goes to Blandine.)

Ah, it's the audacious one.

(Two furious lions rush into the arena; the gladiator attacks them, puts the first to flight and engages the second, hand to hand. They disappear for a moment then the gladiator returns dragging the cadaver of a lion which he casts at Blandine's feet. An immense approval rises from all sides.)

ALL

Mercy! Mercy!

TIBERIUS (aside)

This crowd is stupid.

ALL

Mercy, Caesar, mercy.

TIBERIUS

Respect for the customs of Rome! It's not Caesar who has the right of mercy in the amphitheatre, it's the Grand Vestal. If she remains seated it's death. If she rises it's pardon.

(The Grand Vestal rises to renewed acclamations)

So be it. Tiberius has no more to do than than to accede. Blandine will live.

(To Gladiator)

But you, who are you, really?

(The Gladiator pushes back his helmet revealing Vindex.)

It was him!

(Blandine throws herself in the arms of Vindex.

TIBERIUS

Tiberius, that they accuse of being a tyrant, insists on giving proof of personal humility and submission to the laws. Not even the Emperor has the right to do justice himself. Therefor, it's to the courts of Rome that I hand over Nerva and his accomplices. Vindex is one of them. Separate hi9m from that woman.

(They rush Vindex and drag him away.)

VINDEX

Blandine, Blandine, who wuill protect you now.

(Blandine raises her hand and points to heaven.)

TIBERIUS

I defy your god!

CURTAIN

ACT IV

SCENE V: UNCLE AND NEPHEW

Caligula's room in the palace of Capri. A large door at the back opening on a gallery; a door on one side, on the other a terrace with a garden.

AT RISE, several young women dance before Caligula who nonchalantly stretches on a purple cushion and accompanies them with castanets. Albin stands behind him.

CALIGULA

Enough, my beautiful dancers. Sweat pours on your faces like dew on flowers. Go rest now in the shade of myrtles and turpentine trees. Caius is pleased with you. Wriggling vipers, flexible adders, capricious salamanders. Caius thanks yopu and he regrets his sad condition of languor doesn't allow him to play his role in the ballet of Turnus that you just danced before him. Go—and so that the poor sick man will be happy tomorrow offer a sacrifice to Terpsichore the agile Goddess.

(The dancers leave.)

Do you find, Albin, that I've made progress playing Castanets?

ALBIN

Enormous, Lord.

CALIGULA

I also need to play the flute—it's a delightful instrument!

(Throwing away the castanets.)

Do you think that my uncle will consent to give me a music master to teach me the flute?

ALBIN

I don't doubt it, Lord.

CALIGULA

My uncle Tiberius is so nice—yet, I wouldn't dare to ask him for this favor myself. Would you like to take care of it?

ALBIN

Joyfully, Lord.

CALIGULA

Thanks! Hold on, in the Ballet of Turnus there's a charming step that begins like this (dancing) Oof! I cannot continue. I lack the breath, and my week legs won't support me.

(He falls back on his cushions.)Ah, I'm really sick.

(coughing)

What a frightful cough, right? Do you hear that nasty noise in my left lung?

ALBIN

You will get better, my Lord. My cares will be stronger than the illness.

CALIGULA

Oh, sure. It won't be your fault if I die.

ALBIN

Die! What an idea!

CALIGULA

I am really condemned, go! And it's a natural thing while waiting for the final hour that I think a bit to distract myself. Would you like to help me a little?

ALBIN

If it's in my power.

CALIGULA

Yes.

ALBIN

What does my young master desire?

CALIGULA

Ho! Such a small thing—to satisfy a whem, a fantasy.

ALBIN

Speak.

CALIGULA

My ill condition and my uncle's will have prevented me from going to the amphitheatre. I know only by hearsay what took place, and I desire to hear the tale from the mouth of this Gaul himself—the one who killed two lions with two blows of the sword.

ALBIN

But, Lord—

CALIGULA

And lions from the Atlas, they say. Is that true?

ALBIN

It's true.

CALIGULA

To do that requires not only great courage, but great skill.

ALBIN

Vindex is very well known for his.

CALIGULA

Then he's a man who makes a sword do everything he wants.

ALBIN

Everything he wants.

CALIGULA

Of the type that it would be wrong to seek a quarrel with him.

ALBIN

A while ago a legionary took in his head to brave him. "Friend," said Vindex, to him gaily,"you are ill and you need a bleeding." And, after two or three passes he cut his artery as deftly as a surgeon with a scalpel.

CALIGULA (aside)

This is just the man I need.

(To Albin)

Find a way to bring him here without anyone knowing it.

ALBIN

Why that's impossible.

CALIGULA

Why's that?

ALBIN

Because Caesar had him shipped to Rome with Nerva and the other conspirators.

CALIGULA

I think that you are mistaken. Tiberius is keeping Vindex and Blandine at Capri—so you see it is easy for you to bring this Gaul to me. Here, at your belt, the key to his cell.

ALBIN

Lord.

CALIGULA

I am curious to see him. Where's the harm in that?

ALBIN

Tiberius has forbidden me to do it.

CALIGULA

Tiberias.

(Rising abruptly to make sure no one can see him, then returning to Albin.)

Heavens, my good frien, let's cast off our masks. Tiberias has placed you near me to spy on me.

(Reaction by Albin.)

Don't lie!

(He snatches Albin's notebooks)

My words, my actions, even my thoughts are written here.

ALBIN

O great Jupiter.

CALIGULA

Forget Jupiter, and pay careful attention to what I say, Tiberius is master today, but I will be tomorrow. In that case, demonstrate you are a clever man by attaching your fortune to that of a new power, or a stupid slave adoring a decrepit idol—to no profit.

Choose between Tiberius and me!

ALBIN

Much lower, Lord, much lower.

CALIGULA

Choose!

ALBIN (bending his knee)

Your slave awaits your orders.

CALIGULA

You are going to free Vindex from his cfell and lead him here—secretly.

ALBIN

Yes, Lord.

CALIGULA

Once Vinedex enters, you will hide at the bottom of this terrace, behind the orange bushes. If he returns that way, you will stab him! Here comes Tiberius—but don't let him see you, and be sure, before introducing the Gaul, to wait until I am quite alone.

(Albin leaves.)

Tiberius—he suspects me. He's going to spring some trap on me. Possibly, he's decided on my death. Oh, yes. I feel it. I'm reaching the supreme crisis, and I need to marshal all my strength to avoid the peril. One distraction and I ruin myself. One imprudence and I am lost. A false step and I fall to the bottom of the abyss. What perfidy is he preparing? What trap is going to open beneath my feet? From what side will his blows come? With Tiberius one can never know anything, guess anything in advance. And yet, I must defend myself when the attack comes. Oh, atrocious life—when one has unbridled ambition, ungratified youth, ardent thirst for power—in the end the empiure of the world is the prize, to whoever feigns best, dear uncle.

(He takes the castanets and begins to dance.)

TIBERIUS (entering, aside)

Now there's my most dangerous enemy, and the hour has come to read to the depth of his most secret thoughts.

(aloud)

Bravo, my handsome nephew, bravo!

CALIGULA

Pardon, Caesar, I thought I was alone, I was studying.

TIBERIUS

What precision! What lightness—Do you know you will soon be capable of competing in the theatre of Pompey?

CALIGULA

Why—if Tiberius deigns to permit me.

TIBERIUS

You, an actor! Come on! You are just trying to find a pretext to leave Capri where you amuse yourself, and return to Rome where you have so many friends.

CALIGULA

Oh—could you possibly think?

TIBERIUS

Indeed, I think you have great intentions to play a comedy.

(A silence.)

Who would you actually see in Rome?

CALIGULA

Not many people.

TIBERIUS

Again—

CALIGULA

Cythicus, the character at the Circus. The one who popularized Greek-style contests—a charming man, and an enthusiast for Tiberius.

TIBERIUS

That's a great honor for Tiberius—and then?

CALIGULA

The musician Cherea, who's just invented a very ingenious hydraulic organ. Aesop, the great tragedian, and Apelles, the clever director of the Theatre of Balbus. Allow me to speak first of my friend Cherea?

TIBERIUS

No—there are too many musicians in Rome. I've got the whole racket in loathing and I'll end by putting it in good order.

CALIGULA

Caesar who is the protector of belles0lettres doubtl;ess knows Aesop.

TIBERIUS

That bawler of tragedies who is, they say, the last partisan of sacred traditions?

CALIGULA

It's true. A fanatic enemy of innovators he won't hear talk of bears, or hunts, or ballets or battles in the theatre. He insists that the mise-en-scene absorb thought, replace invention—and that in our days the mechanic kills the poet. He shouts with all his lungs that the noise of horses and dogs and luxurious decorations are the complete decadence of dramatic art. Finally, he is still, the dear man, for pure Greek Tragedy, for the clever comedy of Menander, and it's actually with pain that he accepts Plautus and Terence! As for the director of the Theatre of Balbus, the proud and despotic Apelles—

TIBERIUS

A sort of Caesar in his profession.

CALIGULA

Contrary to Aesop he is the partisan of all bold new things, he puts on stage the cadavers of men and animals, heaped up pell-mell, he wants waves and real flames, and it's at his place that finally—in the Burning of Afranius—the fire reached the hall where numerous spectators were burned—but the play caused a furor—

TIBERIUS (aside)

What inoffensive babbling—

CALIGULA

Ah, the theatre! It's the great business, the great passion of Rome today.

TIBERIUS

Agreed—and as for me, I love the theatre—but still cannot spend all one's time there, and far from me you must have other distractions

CALIGULA

I would go, every day, to the Capena gate—that elegant rendez-vous of opulence and the nobility of Rome—it's a very elegant place to look at Senators draped in purple strolling in liters, knights coming in with their hunting outfits, officers of the PraetorianGuard prancing their Arab horses; in the heavy rhedas harnessed to mules covered with blades of gold and precious stones, on which are stretched veiled matrons crossing themselves with the light Cisium, where the Greek Courtesans, dressed in splendid clothes herself escorts her lovers. Busy looking everywhere I galloped as far as the first tomb on the Appian way—and night came.

TIBERIUS

Night came.

CALIGULA

I'd disguised myself in a long robe and a wig with other kids like me, and we would make an uproar on the Milvian bridge.

TIBERIUS

Very fine. But when it rains?

CALIGULA

In that case I wouldn't leave my stables where the Charioteer Cythicus would teach me a the best ways of caring for my horse.

TIBERIUS

Noble and touching study—

CALIGULA

And then—

TIBERIUS

Ah—there's an "and then."

CALIGULA

I would try, as is the fashion to compose some bad verse.

TIBERIUS

Yes, but you are not speaking to me of women? Well, you are blushing—

CALIGULA

Because—

TIBERIUS

Because?

CALIGULA

I don't like them.

TIBERIUS

Oh, charming naivety of youth. Is there still such innocence in the world? Alas, it's sad to say, my poor Caligula, you must soon renounce these pass-times. As candid as they are childish—for sure, but not worthy of the successor of Tiberius,

CALIGULA

O my uncle, my master—don't give me that name.

(Caligula starts to cry.)

TIBERIUS (aside)

It's unheard of with what ease he weeps.

(aloud)

Now there are tears which prove a good heart and I remember having shed such each time Augustus spoke to me of his approaching end, and my ascension to the empire. One can really see you are of my blood. Do you know there is a great similarity in our destinies? I was the heir of

Augustus, you are mine. But the crown will come to you naturally, while I had to conquer it. Ah, what a struggle, my friend, what refinements of prudence, what a series of dangers and terrors, what feverish shaking of the tortured exile. Luckily, I understood my role, right away. It was belittling myself basely, to stunt myself as much as possible, to feign a bestial terror, a stupid debility, so as not to ruin myself—I almost went to the point of degrading myself. Indeed, Caius, do you know much about my life?

CALIGULA

I only know what Caesar has deigned to teach me.

TIBERIUS

Listen up then, I'm in an effusive mood. As long as Augustus lived I led the most wretched existence; I no longer wore the toga, I renounced the exercise of arms, I didn't even ride a horse. I carefully avoided looks, visits, discussions, and I even went so far as to ask the master to place a guardian near me to observe my actions, so as to assure him that I wasn't plotting—you understand clearly, don't you? Doubtless you would have done the same?

CALIGULA (aside)

The vulture narrows his circling.

TIBERIUS

Finally, the death of Augustus gave me the throne, and I must have heirs in my turn. I would have had too many. I won't spek to you from memory of the grandson of Augustus, Agrippa who was killed in prison. I protested solemnly that I wasn't there—uselessly and there was no question of it. I arrive immediately to Germanicus, to your father. He was a victorious warrior, a magnificent prince that was called a hero, to say it all—and behold in the midst of a triumphal tour through the provinces he died suddenly—the general rumor was he had been poisoned.

CALIGULA

Yes, by Piso.

TIBERIUS

Piso was only an instrument, the blow came from another.

CALIGULA

From whom?

TIBERIUS

From me!—What do you say about that?

CALIGULA

The life of subjects belongs to the master!

TIBERIUS

But he was your father!

CALIGULA

He was your enemy!-

TIBERIUS

Let's skip that. After having for some time howled every night under my windows, "Give us back Germanicus," the Roman people bored with the serenade, and, as is the custom, made another choice, so as not to lack idols, this time it adopted the whole family! Ah, one fine day in which one fine day, in which I myself recognized the six children of heroes ! They hugged each other, shed tears of joy over it—it was a general softening up, and like a return to the Golden Age! Mad illusions!They counted without death which was always for me an intelligent auxiliary, and indeed of the six fine heirs, a short time later only three remained. Look at me carefully,—you seem moved, trembling.

CALIGULA

I don't think of being so.

(Tiberius takes his hand excitedly.)

TIBERIUS (aside)

No—nothing.

(aloud)

All the same, I wouldn't consider this fraternal pride a crime in you.

CALIGULA

Did I weep for my father?

TIBERIUS

So—only three children remained. Nero, Drusus and you. Nero died first on the isle of Pontus, and Drusus, the one of your brothers that you loved the most—after having suffered all the tortures of hunger in the depth of his cell, expired, devouring the straw in his mattress.

(aside)

Still nothing. Face of marble where not a muscle quivers.

(aloud)

The assassin they pointed fingers at was Sejanus—but Sejanus, like Piso before him had only obeyed—the order came from another.

CALIGULA

From whom?

TIBERIUS

From me.

CALIGULA

He didn't deserve mercy because he conspired.

TIBERIUS

As for your mother—ah, you shake this time, I saw it.

CALIGULA

Let Tiberius deign top take my pulse and see if my heart beats harder.

TIBERIUS

Child! Why choke off this cry of nature. She loved you so much, this good mother. She had so many tender caresses for you—myself, you see, me, Tiberius, who did her so much harm, I miss her often, and I never speak of her without emotion. Ah, she was a true matron, chaste, faithful to her husband, as worthy of admiration as of love, and resplendent with ancient virtues, after having seen this modern Niobe, all her children fell around her under blows of invincible arrows. She killed herself in despair, and from her dying mouth escaped a final sob—a last kiss, a last blessing for her beloved Caius!

(aside)

Nothing, still nothing—hand icy, lips motionless, dry eyed, he who weeps so easily.

(aloud)

It's wrong not to miss this mother.

CALIGULA

I did miss her.

TIBERIUS

Ah!

CALIGULA

But, I told myself she would have expressed more love for me by staying alive—and besides—wouldn't I be an ingrate to pity myself, when it's you who replace all my family?

TIBERIUS

In the end, today, I have no other heir than you.

CALIGULA

What do you conclude from that?

TIBERIUS

I've concluded that you too, must died

CALIGULA

I am ready.

TIBERIUS

We'll see about that! Under Augustus there were two Tiberiuses. The false was the one who marched, who spoke, who had the gift of tears, who protested his devotion! The true, that was never seen, was always hidden behind the other! Under Tiberius, there are two Caligulas—the false one who feigns being ill, who dances to his castanets, who speaks only of the theatre, who lives with charioteers and actors, who stays with his horse on rainy days—the true one, he's the one who lies, who conspires, who hates me, who dreams of usurpation, and murder—and who is going to die!

CALIGULA

I said I was ready.

TIBERIUS

Help me, Narses!

(Narses appears.)

TIBERIUS

Draw your sword and kill my nephew Tiberius.

NARSES

Lord?

TIBERIUS

Obey!

CALIGULA

Strike, Narses, strike to the heart! There's never been one more devoted, more loyal! I call the Gods to witness that I have not one sin, not even one bad thought to reproach myself with against Tiberius. The only favor I ask of them is to one day confound slander and enlighten my benefactor about this poor little Caius who loved him so much!

TIBERIUS

Obey, will you!

(Narses raises his sword.)

Stop! It was only a test!

CALIGULA

O joy! You believe in my innocence. You give me back your confidence.

TIBERIUS

Let's not go to work so fast, test, let's wait a bit.

NARSES

Caesar, in the great hall there's a deputation from Smyrna and from eleven towns in Asia.

TIBERIUS

What do these brave folks want?

NARSES

They are contesting for the honor of raising a temple to you and praying that you yourself will choose the location.

TIBERIUS

A temple! But I've already said that I am not a god and that I don't want to be a god! These adulations beset me in the end! A temple? It's Smyrna that I would choose from preference—but, yet once agasin, I do not want a temple, I will never consent to be adored. In the end, from politeness, I'm going to listen to their reasons. Au-revoir, Caius, au-revoir!

(Casting a final glance at him)

Ah, he could mislead Tiberius himself.

(Tiberius leaves with Narses.)

CALIGULA

I paid for audacity, but I almost gave myself away, and I truly thought I was lost! To have deceived Tiberius once more. That's something. But the danger will revive in an hour—more terrible, perhaps! Yes, my calculation was correct when I gave the order to bring this Gaul to me—and I have no other means of salvation. Nothing is done until I've torn from the mind of Tiberius the last suspicion—until I've given irrefutable proof of my devotion? The method I am employing is complicated, buizarre, extravagant—but I'm convinced it will succeed My adversary is not one who can be caught in vulgar snares.

(Looking about outside.)

No one. Marvelous.

ALBIN (appearing)

He's here.

CALIGULA

Show him in.

ALBIN (to Vindex)

This way.

VINDEX (aside)

Caius? What's he want with me?

CALIGULA (low to Albin)

Stand guard on the terrace now. You recall my instructions?

ALBIN

Perfectly.

(Albin leaves.)

CALIGULA (to Vindex)

Approach, friend, I love brave people and I wish you well.

VINDEX

Do you have need of me?

CALIGULA

Will you accept if it's an exchange?

VINDEX

First of all—let's see what you are offering me.

CALIGULA

Your liberty.

VINDEX

That's very little.

CALIGULA

That of Blandine's with yours.

VINDEX

You can give me Blandine?

CALIGULA

Yes.

VINDEX

How?

CALIGULA

I bribed her jailors and I had the young girl taken to the sea-shore where a ship awaits the two of you. Are you satisfied?

VINDEX

Not yet.

CALIGULA

You want to blackmail me, from what I can see.

VINDEX

I am a Gaul, and you are a Roman. I'm treating you as a conquered country.

CALIGULA

So what are you asking?

VINDEX

Nerva's liberty.

CALIGULA

But he's no longer in Capri.

VINDEX

I know it.

CALIGULA

Well then?

VINDEX

Write the magistrates to open the gates of the prison for him.

CALIGULA

The magistrates only obey Tiberius and would regard my letter as of no account.

VINDEX

What does it matter to you if I am satisfied? Not being able to have the signature of Tiberius, I will take yours.

CALIGULA

After all, it's your affair.

(After having written)

Here it is. I hope it's worded in terms urgent enough.

VINDEX

While you are holding the pen, write another thing.

CALIGULA

What?

VINDEX

A safe conduct to Gaul.

CALIGULA

Gladly.

VINDEX

Leave blank the name and the number of persons who can use it.

CALIGULA

Nothing simpler.

(aside)

I can promise anything.

VINDEX

Fine!

(as he reads, Caligula approaches the window)

Are you there?

ALBIN (outside)

Yes, Lord.

CALIGULA

After you've killed him bring me back the written documents I've just given him.

VINDEX

To whom are you speaking?

CALIGULA

To the man who's charged to take you to Blandine. I'm telling him we are in agreement.

VINDEX

You are in too great a hurry. Because I've not yet accepted the bargain, and you've just shown yourself so easily generous that in truth it shocks me. I'm afraid that you are asking me something impossible.

CALIGULA

On the contrary, nothing could be simpler.

VINDEX

I'm listening.

CALIGULA

You are not only a clever arms maker, but an excellent fencing master—and they say you use marvelously the swords you forge.

VINDEX

They say true.

CALIGULA

If we crossed swords, you would be master enough with your sharp eye and your sword to give me a wound—terrible in appearance. But which would not place my life in danger.

VINDEX

I'll answer for it.

CALIGULA

How would you do it?

VINDEX

I would give the blow to the breast, but instead of pushing straight, I would make the weapon slide in the flesh. At first, they would think you lost. But, in a week you would be cured.

CALIGULA

That's fine; you are a precious man. Now that's the service I demand of you.

VINDEX

I suppose you've lost your head.

CALIGULA

In short you accept?

VINDEX

First, swear to me that Blandine is free and that you are not deceiving me.

CALIGULA

By what do you want me to swear? By the lance of Mars, by the spear of Minerva, the Egyptian crocodile, Ibis, fattened with serpents, the Golden Monkey with the long tail. You have a long choice there are more gods in heaven than men on earth.

VINDEX

Tiberius hides his impiety, Caius makes a parade of it.

CALIGULA

These Gauls are so solemn! Copme on, I swear by interests!

VINDEX

The oath is bizarre, but I accept it. It's the only one coming from Caius that could be since.

CALIGULA (looking out the window)

An oath for formality.

(aloud)

As for me, I have so much confidence in you that I ask nothing.

VINDEX

You do well; men of my race don't stoop to deceive.

CALIGULA

Now detach two swords from this panoply. I take one, you take the other. When you have wounded me, throw yours away and flee.

VINDEX

Which way?

CALIGULA

By the terrace. It's the only way which may be safe, which can lead you from rock to rock to the shore of the sea. Someone's coming. En garde!

(They cross swords)

And strike when I tell you.

VINDEX

The click of iron animates me, and when I have at the end of my sword opne of the implacable enemies of my race, I need all my control not to kill you without pity.

CALIGULA

Now, now—think of our agreement.

VINDEX

Don't worry.

CALIGULA

Strike!

(Vindex wounds him.)

Ah, the wiseacre has a heavy hand; leave quickly.

(calling)

Help! Help!

VINDEX

Oh, to see her, to save her.

(As he starts to leave by the terrace Kiomara opens a side door and stops him.)

KIOMARA (quick and low)

Wretch! That way is death. Come!

(She drags him away by the door she opened. Tiberius and his suite erupt from the hall.)

TIBERIUS (along with Narses, Albin, slaves, and the deputation from Smyrna)

What's happening here. Caius, wounded.

CALIGULA

Caesar, I surprised the Gaul Vindex who came to assassinate you. We fought. He fled by this terrace.

TIBERIUS

Run! Let him be brought to me!

(Narses rushes out with some Praetorians.)

CALIGULA

I'm choking. I cannot say more. I've given my life to save you.

TIBERIUS

Real blood! A real wound!

(To a Doctor)

Take all possible care of my poor nephew.

(To Albin)

Don't let this event be noised about too much.

(aside)

That would make him even more popular.

(To Caligula)

Well, my poor child—

CALIGULA

Dying for Caesar, I die happy!

(He faints.)

TIBERIUS

Such devotion. Have I really been deceived on his accfount? Was he really only a ninny?

ALBIN

Caesar.

TIBERIUS

What is it now?

ALBIN

The envoys from Smyrna request to take their leave of Caesar.

TIBERIUS

Let them enter.

(Albin introduces the envoys)

Hide the wounded better, will you!

(aloud)

Return to Smyrna, honest citizens. You are going to erect a temple to me. I've allowed you to do it. It's agreed. I don't go back on my word. But I protest

Before you all, you've done violence to our imperial modesty.

ALL

Long live Tiberius.

TIBERIUS (aside)

Come on—here I am God!

CURTAIN

SCENE VI

THE IMPERIAL CAVERN

The bedroom of Tiberius full of soldiers and courtiers. Tiberius paces around with agitation, and stops before the Doctor who has just entered.

TIBERIUS (to Doctor)

Well?

DOCTOR

Fever, Caesar, lot's of fever, but the wound is less dangerous than we thought at first.

TIBERIUS

I've suspected that a little.

(aside)

The trickster lacks frankness even in his wounds.

(aloud)

In that case there's no danger of death?

DOCTOR

No, Caesar.

TIBERIUS

What do you know about it?

DOCTOR

Why—science.

TIBERIUS

Stupidity and vanity. Doctors are all the sdame with their pretenses of infallibility—as if they were the sole arbiters of human life. I tell you no one is ever sure of anything.

DOCTOR

Caesar—

TIBERIUS

In short, I see no obstacle that he live. Bad people shan't accuse me of having killed him like the others. Go back to him. Ah, listen, still. If he gets delirious, send for me.

(aside)The most tricky betray themselves at such moments.

(The doctor leaves)

I really believe I've got proof that Caius was struck by another hand than his—he accuses the Gaul who has indeed disappeared from prison. There's where they mystery begins. I don't know yet why they haven't caught Vindex. Why hasn't it been done already?

(Rushing to Narses who enters.)

Finally—where is he?

NARSES

May Caesar punish me—because despite all our efforts we've yet to find anyone.

TIBERIUS

I have to have him. I have to have him dead or alive.

KIOMARA (entering)

Let Caesar deign to wait until tomorrow.

TIBERIUS

Why?

KIOMARA

I was climbing Mount Solaro to pick plants that give sleep when I saw Vindex flee through the rocks near the sea. Then suddenly, he lost his footing and rolled into the abyss. Tomorrow the waves will cast his body back onto the shore.

TIBERIUS

Let them watch the beach carefully. I insist on seeing the body.

(Abruptly giving to all present their dismissal. To Kiomara)

You're not deceiving me?

KIOMARA

Where'd you get that idea from?

TIBERIUS

From the fact that Vindex's country is yours.

KIOMARA

A slave has no country.

TIBERIUS

I had you sought vainly since yesterday. And that makes me believe you've taken care to avoid me so as not to answer my questions.

KIOMARA

Concerning what?

TIBERIUS

By whom was Vindex able to get into the amphitheatre and obtain weapons?

KIOMARA

By me.

TIBERIUS

You admit it?

KIOMARA

Nothing simpler. It's a custom to make use of Caesar's prisoners in the circus games, and, having no orders to the contrary for this man, I let him mix with the other gladiators.

TIBERIUS

We'll see about it later. In short, where were you all the time?

KIOMARA

I remained on the summits to observe the stars.

TIBERIUS

Ah—what did they announce.

KIOMARA

Great, and soon to come events.

TIBERIUS

Lucky or unlucky?

KIOMARA

I dopn't know yet.

TIBERIUS

When will you know?

KIOMARA

This very night.

TIBERIUS

And I will be forewarned.

KIOMARA

The first of all. Sleep well, Caesar.

(She leaves slowly.)

TIBERIUS (alone)

Yet another night is going to pass. Oh, I don't like nights, they are so long. There are still creatures who can sleep until morning without waking, without dreaming. —Let's think of something else. So—I'm going to have a temple in Smyrna? How will that get me ahead? I don't think so. These poor gods are going to be very weary, new ones need to be manufactured to forget the old. God! Are there really any? My reason refuses to believ it. Still, if there were—not several—but a single one who was listening to me at this moment—yes, a sole one. Bah—which?

(violent lightning clap)

Poor human nature. It doesn't bel;ieve in gods but is afraid of thunder. Heaven was so pure just now. How quietly this storm declared itself. It only thunders on the left—luckily—a frightful noise—imprudent, I don't have my laurel crown.

(He puts it on his head)

There. Now I no longer fear the thunder. I don't want to see those flashes of lightning. Suppose I tried to sleep. Yes, that's the thing. But, first of all, am I quite alone?

I have to make sure. Someone could be hiding here.

(After having toured the room he lies down on his bed.)

The storm's a long way off. Let's sleep.

(A silence.)

And power! As soon as I close my eyes for a moment terrible visions dance nad grimace before me in a sinister half lighrt. It's the hour, in which, they say, the dead come back from the cemetery as Lamias. The dead! Are these ghosts? No, I would have seen them already. But can I see them?

(calling)

Lighrts, lights.

(Romulus enters bearing a lamp.)

TIBERIUS (aside)

A little flaming oakum in the hands of an imbecile. Now there's something to reassure Tiberius.

(aloud)

Ah, indeed. How is it you are still alive?

ROMULUS

Thanks to Caesar's clemency.

TIBERIUS

I don't recall it.

ROMULUS

Yesterday, Caesar, yesterday. When they decked me out as a gladiator. You laughed so much that it was worth my pardon.

TIBERIUS

It's true. I even told Narses to employ you in the palace.

ROMULUS

Narses put me in charge of the imperial lamps. But it's up to Caesar to appoint a more suitable duty for me.

TIBERIUS

You're becoming demanding—indeed. Serve me as a buffoon.

ROMULUS

O joy! My hands will no longer feel oily.

TIBERIUS

Enter your functions immediately.

ROMULUS

How?

TIBERIUS

Make me laugh.

ROMULUS

Make you laugh?

TIBERIUS

Well, yes, like yesterday.

ROMULUS

But I'm no longer rigged out as a gladiator.

TIBERIUS

A clown has more than one grimace in his sack. Tery something else. And hurry up. But I warn you: you will have great trouble to cheer me up.

ROMULUS

And if I don't succeed in my efforts?

TIBERIUS

I'll give you to Pyhton.

ROMULUS

Who is this Python?

TIBERIUS

My favorite serpent, a magnificent boa-constrictor

ROMULUS

A boa-?

TIBERIUS

The one who already ate your predecessor.

ROMULUS

Great Gods.

TIBERIUS

I don't coddle comedians, inpertinent rogues who accept without hesitation the difficult task of cheering up Tiberias.

ROMULUS

Caesar, nice Caesar, give me back my lamps. It's a modest profession which better suits my tastes.

TIBERIUS

It's too late.

ROMULUS

I will overcome the horror I have for oil. I consent to poison my fingers.

TIBERIUS

Python's famished, do you hear? His cage is there in the wall—hurry up, or I'll open it.

ROMULUS

Wait, Caesar, wait. You are going to laugh. Poor Romulus—to be eaten quickly. I sing, I dance, I invent grimaces. You see, I'm douing all I can. Must I walk on my hands, balance on the top of a hcair, swallow a sword, imitate the screams of a blackbird? I don't know any more. I'm sweating, I'm going crazy. Pity, Caesar, pity.

(Turning towards the wall designated by Tiberius.)

Shut up. Villainous beast.

TIBERIUS

Come on, get up, I smiled. Python wikll wait until tomorrow.

ROMULUS (aside)

Why, this is not a life!

(aloud)

Then, I can retire?

TIBERIUS

No, you will spend the night with me.

(aside)

I won't be alone.

ROMULUS (aside)

So long as the cage doesn't open—by itself. Let's crouch down here.

TIBERIUS

Oh, if I could sleep

ROMULUS

A Jewish Rabbi recently told me the story of Jonas in the belly of the whale. My position is nearly the same. Except the ending threatens to be more tragic for me: to be the lunch or suopper of a Boa-. He's sleeping, the tyrant. Yes, I believe he's sleeping. Oh, old rogue, if I dared.

(Kiomara enters holding a cup in her hand)

Now what's this.

(He hides.)

KIOMARA (aside)

The hour has come.

(She looks at Tiberius who tosses in his bed, utters a choked cry and wakes with a start.)

TIBERIUS

Ah, shocking dream.

KIOMARA

Caesar's sleep is quite agitated.

TIBERIUS

I saw the Mausoleum of Augustus open and from it emerge a voice which called me by name—then I don't know what—something white, veiled, bloody, advanced towards me, shouting three times:"Beware!" A moment later the statues of the fourteen nations of the empire shook, falling from their pedestals and came to floor me. At last I felt myself covered by a multitude of ants—which gnawed my skull and devoured my heart.

KIOMARA

Tiberius, frightened of a dream?

TIBERIUS

You don't believe in dreams?

KIOMARA

No. Mad visions, incoherent chimeras, products of chance that truth contradicts.

TIBERIUS

Still, those ants worry me. Fear the multitude—they are powerful.

KIOMARA

Banish, will you, fears unworthy of you. This beverage contains the juice of herbs gathered by me on Mount Solaro and will preserve Caesar from insomnia.

TIBERIUS (avidly)

In that case give it to me.

KIOMARA

Wait till I have the cup tested.

TIBERIUS

No, it's unnecessary. I'm not suspicious of you, my faithful slave. Give it to me. Ah, I'm broken. I really need to sleep.

(After drinking it he falls motionless into his bed.)

KIOMARA

Sleep, will you.

(She places her hand on his heart.)

The effect of the thunder.

(She introduces Vindex.)

Come, you are going to learn what sacered bonds join us together.

ROMULUS

Heavens, it's my friend the Barbarian.

VINDEX

Woman, I don't know the mysterious and terrible work that you are going to accomplish, but I abandon myself to you, blindly. You've returned Blandine to me.

ROMULUS

Psst!

KIOMARA

A man here!

(She pulls a dagger.)

VINDEX

Romulus. I'll answer for him.

KIOMARA

But he's a Roman!

VINDEX (smiling)

I think he clings less to that title since his voyage to Capr.

(to Romulus)

Right?

ROMULUS

I'll answer for it.

KIOMARA

Then let him shut up and obey.

ROMULUS

Oh, I really want to.

KIOMARA

Carry this sleeping old geezer.

ROMULUS

Tiberius

KIOMARA

Yes, the master of the world!

ROMULUS (to Vindex)

Let me take his feet. I prefer that.

KIOMARA (taking the lamp)

Now follow me!

CURTAIN

SCENE VII

THE GAULS IN CAPRI

Immense subterranean vaults connected to each other by gigantic pillars. At the back, a huge sheet of dormant water half drowned in fog.

VINDEX

Tiberius still hasn't woken up.

ROMULUS

He hasn't made a reaction since we placed him on this block of rocks. But in the end, where are we?

VINDEX

I don't know any more than you. We'll soon learn from Kiomara who ought to come find us.

ROMULUS

This place must be swarming with reptiles and wild beasts. —An idea!

VINDEX

What?

ROMULUS

Suppose this is the subterranean manageries of Tiberius?

VINDEX

Eternal trembler that you are.

ROMULUS

A braver man would at least be afraid.

VINDEX

When one conspires, one must expect adventures.

ROMULUS

Yes, but there are too many already. —Not counting those that still await me. And to say that it's the fault of my old usurer of a landlord.

VINDEX

What do you mean?

ROMULUS

No question. Had he no0t demanded money, I would be sleeping at this hour calmly in my little room, and tomorrow morning on waking, I would have a hello from my neighbor, a fat lower class woman whose hair is always messy and jolly.

Cursed politics, go. How far you lead us—ambitious ones like us.

VINDEX

To tell you the truth, my poor Romulus, I doubt you'll ever see your garret again, or me, my shop.

ROMULUS

You have a way of reassuring people.

VINDEX

After all, who knows? Hasn't heaven already saved us from the fury of Tiberius and his lions? And, while waiting for Kiomara, let's explore this underground a bit.

ROMULUS

Don't leave me, barbarian friend, don't leave me.

VINDEX

Decidedly, you would have made a bad soldier.

ROMULUS

I didn't have to cut my skin to escape military service. Citizens of Rome are exempt by law.

VINDEX

Isn't that water that's shining over there?

ROMULUS

It's quite possible.

VINDEX

Yes, a great lake with dormant waves.

ROMULUS

Suppose it were the Styx or the Acheron ? If we were to go see it appear. Ah, look over that way.

VINDEX

I cannot make anything out.

ROMULUS

I tell you I just saw a huge face slide by—all white.

VINDEX

It's the effect of fear.

ROMULUS

No—wait—again.

VINDEX

Indeed!

ROMULUS

Ghosts, they are ghosts,—we are lost.

VINDEX

Silence, will you.

ROMULUS

And there, that reddish light.

VINDEX

One would say it's the light of a torch.

ROMULUS

Walking by itself.

VINDEX

Here's Kiomara.

(Kiomara is draped in a great cloak of similar color.)

KIOMARA

Roman, leave us alone.

ROMULUS

And where do you want me to go?

KIOMARA

Where you please.

(pointing)

Over there.

ROMULUS

That's where the ghosts are.

KIOMARA (pointing in a different direction)

There.

ROMULUS

That's where the torches are walking.

KIOMARA

Well then, withdraw into the ship.

ROMULUS

What ship?

KIOMARA

That one over there—on the lake.

ROMULUS

And how to reach it? As for me, I don't know how to swim.

KIOMARA

The path that snakes along the rocks will lead you straight there.

ROMULUS

Is your ship inhabited?

KIOMARA

Yes.

ROMULUS

By beings of flesh and blood?

KIOMARA

You will find Nerva's daughter there.

VINDEX

Blandine. Friend, don't leave her—and if danger threatens her protect her even unto death, or better yet, let out a shout and I will go myself.

ROMULUS

That's it, I'll scream. I prefer to scream. Don't worry, you will hear me, I have excellent lungs. By this path, you say? How narrow it is! How slippery!

KIOMARA

Will you go!

ROMULUS

Don't push; I'm leaving. Alas, poor Romulus. How will all this end for you?

(Romulus leaves.)

KIOMARA

Now the two of us, Vindex.

(She throws back her cloak and appears dressed in black, crowned with oak leaves, and wearing a sickle of gold that hangs from her belt.)

VINDEX

This costume.

KIOMARA

It's that of the Druidesses of Gaul, the one that I wore in my pure and strict youth, in the shade of our prophetic oaks, but then Vindex was white like mountaintop snow. Today, slave of shame and dishonor, I can only dress in the clothes of mourning. You are scarcelu listening to me.

VINDEX

Oh, you are mistaken, and your words have moved me deeply, but I am worried despite myself. For what reason have you separated me from Blandine?

KIOMARA

She cannot be present at what is going to take place here.

VINDEX

Swear to me again that she is in no danger.

KIOMARA

Ah, why must you love her?

VINDEX

Woman!

KIOMARA

You haven't escaped the Roman corruption; your masters have not been able to besmirch either your body or your soul, despite them you kept courage, strength, probity, still you would have remained completely worthy of your ancestors without this love that I reproach you for because it is your only weakness. Vindex, you must love only your country.

VINDEX

Vindex loves Gaul, too.

KIOMARA

Not enough, since you give it for a rival the daughter of an enemy race!

VINDEX

Blandine is innocent of the crimes of Rome. Bersides, what are you concerned about? Sghe can only be a foreigner to me. She doesn't love me.

KIOMARA

In that case tear her from your heart.

VINDEX

She already has an altar there.

KIOMARA

Renounce this love.

VINDEX

Never!

KIOMARA

Ah, I have a presentiment that it will be fatal to us. Now I regret having saved her. I would have done better to kill her!

VINDEX

Wretched woman!

KIOMARA

Vindex, you are threatening your sister!

VINDEX

You?

KIOMARA

Your sister, friend, your elder sister, almost your mother! Oh, you didn't see my joy, yesterday, when your birth was revealed to us. You don't know that I almost lacked the strength to repress a scream—so as not to betray myself. Is it possible that you do not recall anything of the past, that you don't find some place in your memory, the look, the sound of my voice, the features of all those who loved you?

VINDEX

No—nothing.

KIOMARA

It's true. You were still so young when misfortune and death separated us from each other. It's still towards me that your little arms turned most often! Many times I cradled you on my knees during our camps in the war; many times I watched you sleep, peaceful and smiling at the nocturnal hour in which bulls, butchered by the hundreds by our priests mooed their last bellowing with the uproar of the storm.

You remember, Vindex, you remember?

VINDEX

Nothing, nothing. Emptiness, shadows.

KIOMARA

One day, it was the end of Autumn, the clouds flew low, a fine rain fell and the North wind shook the heath on an immense plain. All our Gauls under the orders of King Vindex had gone to battle the soldiers of Rome. In the circle of the camp only women and children remained.; motionless, mute, ears to the ground we listened with anxiety to the distant roar of battle. Suddenly, we saw ours fold back, no more doubt, they were defeated. The Roman discipline still carried the day. They approached still, slowly, without ceasing to fight, formidable even in their defeat. But leaving at each step long rows of cadavers. Finally, pursued closely by the conquerors, they reached the fortifications, and rushed in disorder behind this last shelter. —It was then—

VINDEX

Hold on! The veil is leaving, a light pierces the shadows—oh, quite pale, quite distant—

KIOMARA

It was then something horrible and divine took place. Livid, hair in disarray, the Gallic women leapt with furious screams before their husbands and their brothers; they led through the carnage scratching the fleeing with their nails; there were some who rushed like panthers into the midst of the melee, who snatched shields from the Romans and seized swords with their naked hands; others choked their children in a supreme embrace or threw them under the wheel of chariots which ground them into a bloody mud.

VINDEX

Oh—my head's ion fire, my heart leaps to break itself.

KIOMARA

One of them wrapped in a long black veil, a circle of gold on her head, face beautiful and sinister like Volleda, the demi-goddess stood on a pile of cadavers.

VINDEX

Ah, I see her.

KIOMARA

In one arm she held a child, in the other, a dagger. "Romans,: she screamed," you bring to the Gauls steel which enchains, but there's a steel which frees. I don't want my son to be a slave!"

VINDEX

Ah, I see her, I hear her!

KIOMARA

Then she embraced the child for the last time, turned away her eyes and struck him.

VINDEX (opening his tunic)

Here, here!

KIOMARA

Then, withdrawing the fuming weapon she plunged it in her breast, enlarged the wound with her two hands and fell dead.

VINDEX (with a scream)

It was my mother!

KIOMARA

Our mother—who has not been avenged.

VINDEX

She will be!

KIOMARA

Soon!

VINDEX

Continue, sister. I know now that the cares of Nerva recalled me to life. But my father? But you?

KIOMARA

King Vindex dies as a soldier. As for me, I was sold as a slave and I became the mistress of Caesar.

VINDEX

You? You?

KIOMARA

Yes, and it's truly there that my work began. Once at Capri, once ruined, I trampled holy modesty under my feet. I aided the executioners and defied the courtiers, I was crime, shame, impurity, baseness. But all that to ba avenged one day and that day has come.

VINDEX

Didn't you ever have the thought of finishing Tiberius with a dagger blow?

KIOMARA

A thousand times I thought it, a thousand times I could have done it, but it's not the hand of a woman which must strike the monster, it's all Gaul, by the hand of a man—by you, brother.

VINDEX

I am ready!

KIOMARA

Above all, something was needed to seize for me the confidence of Tiberius, and it was difficult, but I succeeded! Tiberius is superstitious and I succeeded in exercising a sort of supernatural domination over him. In an nocturnal excursion that I alone had the right to make freely in Capri, under the pretext of observing the stars and gathering magical herbs, I had the luck of discovering this grotto unkown to all; the plan I am excuting today was conceived in my mind! Ah, the Gods alone can know what I was obliged to employ by way of ruses, vigils, work, years, to pursue my goal through this of espionage and terror extended by Tiberius over the world. But I've finally reached this goal, I've finally reached through this subterranean lake which connects to the sea, I have introduced tonight into the infernal citadel that the tyrant thinks impenetrable to the avengers of my family and country.

VINDEX

To work then!

KIOMARA

Tomorrow, brother a great clamor will shake the Capitol, and echo to the Rhine, and the Euphrates. Where is Tiberius? Find Tiberius! The master of the world will have vanished like a dry leaf in a torrent.

VINDEX

He's waking up.

TIBERIUS

Whera am I? Where am I?

(Kiomara strikes with her gold sickle a shiled suspended from a rock)

KIOMARA

Before your judges.

(The subterranean depth lights up, groups of druids appear on all side.)

TIBERIUS

Ah, this is a shocking dream. Wake me, wake me, will you. I order you to wake me.

KIOMARA

All that you see is real.

TIBERIUS

You lie! Dead! Ghosts!

KIOMARA

Look. I am Kiomara, the Gallic slave.

TIBERIUS

You're a spectre.

KIOMARA

Not at all Tiberius. It's really a living hand which clasps your arm, it's really a living mouth which shows you its laugh!

TIBERIUS

Treachery in that case.

KIOMARA

Justice.;

TIBERIUS

Help me! Help me!

KIOMARA

No one will come.

TIBERIUS

No one!

KIOMARA

No! You belong to us until your last pain, until your last breath.

TIBERIUS

Make way.

(The Druids shake their torches and wave their daggers.)

KIOMARA

Circle of fire and steel!

TIBERIUS

Lost! I am lost!

KIOMARA

Yes! Ah, what joy, what pride to be able to torture slowly with looks, with voice, with gestures the insolent despot who has trampled underfoot the enslaved world, and here he is fallen so low that he'd be pitiful if he weren't Tiberius.

TIBERIUS

But in the end, what do you want?

KIOMARA

Why, I told you already.

TIBERIUS

I don't recall.

KIOMARA

To judge you! Ah, you persecuted our priests, and you boasted of having exterminated them! Well, you see—there remain enough for punishment. Gaul is a fertile mother and our Gods are stronger than yours! You, who knew yourself in vengeance, what do you think of this?

TIBERIUS

Mercy! Mercy!

KIOMARA

I was sure he'd be a coward! Have you ever pardoned so you might be pardoned? Exceutioner of Gaul, be present to learn your sentence.

TIBERIUS

I've gone crazy. I've gone crazy.

FIRST DRUID

Is the sacrifice ready? We have thrown in sacrifice on to the waves of the lake, cakes of wax and the fleece of sheep.

SECOND DRUID

Here's the vase of Water and the iron hand.

THIRD DRUID

The branch of Verbena and two serpents.

FIRST DRUID

I've picked the salomus with my left hand without looking at it, then I made my ablutions, and I left with naked feet to find the sacred moss. In the name of Tarann, the God of Thunder, I ask for the second time if the sacrifice is ready.

KIOMARA

It's waiting.

FIRST DRUID

Then trace the circle and let them plant the sword in the middle. Now, make way for the Priestesses of Vasso!

(Three veiled women enter, howling to the noise of cymbals.)

TIBERIUS

Oh! Horrible vision!

FIRST PRIESTESS

I enter the circle with my sisters who are going to watch like me in the sacred orgies.

SECOND PRIESTESS

We dwell in an island, near Brittany, where no foreigner dares descend. We haunt a forest where the Goddess Hertha strolls every night on naked feet on blood.

THIRD PRIESTESS

The magic cauldron boils nearby and long knives hang from our brass belts.

FIRST DRUID

We are the sons of Tentartes, the Inexorable.

FIRST PRIESTESS

And we are the daughters of Vasso, the genius of destruction, scarcity, earthquakes, bloody meteors, supernatural shades, all come from Vasso! Let's interlace our hands and dance around the sword.

FIRST DRUID

Eubages, bring the white bull.

KIOMARA

The blood of bulls no longer suffices the Gauls. It's human blood they need.

ALL

Human blood!

FIRST DRUID

Who shall we strike? If he's a Gaul, he will lie down on his shield and offer his throat without going pale. Gauls scorn death—for he will find in the land of souls, his horse, his weapons, his battles, and he communicates withthis world through the flames of pyres!

SECOND DRUID

Gauls never fear danger, and never recoil before fire, nor ocean; he pulls his sword against the waves and hurls arrows against thethe tempest.

FIRST DRUID

Shall we immolate a Gaul?

KIOMARA

No—the country doesn't have too many children, Caesar has killed so many. It's a Roman that must die.

FIRST DRUID

Which one?

ALL

Which one?

KIOMARA

The most illustrious and most pitiless of our oppressors. Tiberius.

FIRST DRUID

Where is he?

KIOMARA (pulling Tiberius towards them)

Here he is!

FIRST DRUID

Let him die!

ALL

Yes, yes! Let him die!

TIBERIUS

To die like this! I who have fleets, armies, Rome, the universe.

No, no—it's impossible. I don't want to die! I don't want it! I don't want it!

FIRST DRUID

We are the judges—who will be the executioner?

KIOMARA

The one whom the Gods are sending us!

(Pointing to Vindex)

The son of Vindex, our royal martyr!

(applause)

FIRST DRUID

Make way for the administrator of justice., the one who redresses wrongs.

(Kiomara pulls the sword planted in the circle and gives it to Vindex.)

KIOMARA

To you, the sword!

VINDEX

Give me-

KIOMARA

Avenge you father, avenge your mother, avenge your country.

VINDEX (to Tiberius)

Die then!

TIBERIUS

Mecry! Pity! Not yet! A moment, a mniute, a second.

KIOMARA

Strike!

(Blandine appears, utters a scream, pushes through the crowd and places herself between Vindex and Tiberius.)

VINDEX

Blandine!

KIOMARA

She here!

TIBERIUS

Save me, young girl, you are nice, you have a horror of blood. I kiss your hand. I attach myself to your dress. Save me! Save me!

BLANDINE

Vindex, throw away that weapoin!

KIOMARA (to Blandine)

Get out of here! Leave us alone!

VINDEX

Yes, flee, Blandine, flee this sinister place.

BLANDINE

Vindex, throw away that weapon!

KIOMARA (to Vindex)

But strike, will you!

BLANDINE

You won't kill an old man.

TIBERIUS

An old man. That's well said. A poor old man.

ALL

Death to Tiberius!

VINDEX (to Blandine)

Flee I tell you!

ALL

Death to Tiberius!

BLANDINE

No! Pity! Clemency!

VINDEX

Leave me alone! Leave me alone!

BLANDINE

Yesterday, in the open Circus, in the midst of a crowd avid for carnage, in the face of Caesar, a vestal, a pagan, dared to give you mercy! Will you be more implacable than the idolatrous priestess, you who touched the Cross, you who said to me, "Your God will be mine. "

VINDEX

Blandine!

TIBERIUS

Speak, young girl. Keep talking.

KIOMARA

Vindex! The Gods are getting irritated! Strike will you, strike in the name of your father and your mother, bloody ghosts who have armed your arm!

BLANDINE

Forgive!

KIOMARA

Strike in the name of your sister sold as a slave, and dishonored in a cowardly way.

VINDEX

My sister.

KIOMARA

Strike in the name of your country which will be freed.

VINDEX

Come on! I no longer hesitate!

(He raises his sword over Tiberius who rolls on the ground screaming.)

BLANDINE

Pardon!

(lowering her voice)

I love you.

(Vindex lets his weapon fall.)

KIOMARA

Ah, cowardly heart! Well—

(Kiomara rushes to pick up the sword.)

VINDEX (stopping her)

Those clamors, that noise of arms—

KIOMARA

The Romans have no doubt discovered the subterranean entrance.

(To Druids)

Reach the sea quickly by force of rowing. Leave, brother, leave.

(They extinguish the torches and leave like ghosts.)

As for me, I'll have time to strike him.

(Vindex snatches the weapon and casts it far from her.)

VINDEX

No—it's not to us Tiberius belongs, it's to God. To God alone!

(He drags her away followed by Blandine. Hardly have they gone when a numerous force of soldiers and slaves invade the subterranean. Narses runs to Tiberius, motionless as if fainted.)

NARSES

Deign to rise, Caesar. We are here. You have nothing to fear.

TIBERIUS

Narse, my Praetorians, my slaves.

NARSES

Yes, Caesar, your faithful slaves.

TIBERIUS

Living! I'm still livi9ng. Ah, this is the way it is, wretches, that you watch over my safety, that you allow me to be insulted, that you allow me to be butchered. I will make you see that I am still Caesar!

NARSES

Speak, command. Your enemies wikll be punished!

TIBERIUS

What, traitors, they are not yet?

NARSES

Where to find them?

ALBIN

A trireme loaded with men is fleeing on the lake.

NARSES

Impossible to reach them!

TIBERIUS

A volley of arrows! A volley of arrows!

(Archers fire. After a moment of silence on hears in the distance the shout: "Long live Gaul!")

Clumsies! Again—and aim better!

NARSES

They are very far away. They've reached the sea.

TIBERIUS

Well, if they've escaped me, I've got others in hand. I will go to Rome. I will exterminate all the Gauls found in the city, women as well as men. I will burn their homes, I will have their children thrown into the flames, and if iron, fire, torture, executioners don't suffice to annihilate the sons of this cursed race I will release the four hundred panthers of the Coloseum and the six hundred lions of the great Circus! To Rome!

ALL

To Rome!

CURTAIN

ACT V

SCENE VIII: THE HEIR OF CAESAR

Vast and magnificent gardens. A panorama of Rome lit by setting Sun.

ROMULUS

Here we are arrived, you have nothing to fear here, you will be completely safe to await Procula, that is to say, Vindex—my friend the Barbarian.

BLANDINE

Where have you escorted us to?

ROMULUS

Quite near Rome, you see—to the gardens of Senator Plautus who was recently dragged to the pillory—you remember that night.

BLANDINE

That was the beginning of all my misfortunes.

ROMULUS (aside)

And what about mine! If ever I become a conspirator again—

(aloud)

It's necessary to tell you that I know the property to the tips of my fingers. The deceased was one of my patrons, and I went to greet him at his levees two or three times a week; he was generous enough and always gratified one with some money. It's a great shame for me that died. Anyway, peace to his shade.

BLANDINE

Why does this retreat seem more safe to you than another?

ROMULUS

Because while waiting for the Senate to legally promulgate the edict of confiscation, no one can enter the villa—under the most strict penalties.

BLANDINE

But then—

ROMULUS

It's the best guarantee that no one will come to bother us. And, desides, Vindex cannot long delay his return.

(aside)

If he comes.

(aloud)

Now that you are reassured, I am going to leave you for a moment to run get news.

BLANDINE

Go.

ROMULUS (aside)

Now there's still a Roman citizen of the Gaul and a Druidess. That's politics. Ah, Gods preserve me from ever conspiring.

(Romulus leavers. Blandine goes to Kiomara who has stood aside, somber and thoughtful.)

BLANDINE

Sister.

KIOMARA

That name in your mouth.

BLANDINE

Oh, I give it to you joyfully.

KIOMARA

I am not your sister—I am your enemy.

BLANDINE

You?

KIOMARA

Yes, your enemy.

BLANDINE

Why?

KIOMARA

She asks! Because you destroyed with a single word the work of ten years. My work,—what's more that of which I was proud! And that's not all. In leaving Capri, I was hoping Vindex wouldn't separate from his brothers, but, instead of heading with them towards Gaul, he came to Rome to seek perils without glory, a death without honor! What does vengeance matter? What does country matter?

Do you understand now why I hate you?

BLANDINE

Well, I intend to return that hate to you with affection and tenderness, and devotion. But my trembling hand, my hand that you again reject, seeks you obstinately. And perhaps one day you will love me.

KIOMARA

Never!

BLANDINE

Oh, don't say that.

KIOMARA

Never.

BLANDINE

The future is the secret of God and Vindex will aid me in my sisterly task.

KIOMARA

Vindex, did you say? You are counting on Vindex to bring us together, but don't you know then that the principal cause of my hate is my jealousy! Well, yes, I am jealous like a mother to whom an unknown, a stranger, suddenly comes to steal the tenderness of her child—like a mother wjho has only a second place in the heart she possessed completely? Seeing him again, I felt reborn in me the dearest memories of my past. In this ulcerated soul, bloody, closed to gentle emotions, it awakened a need to love, immense, selfish—and I thought he was going to belong to me unreservedly, this brother, this son, whose first smile I had, the first caresses. There was only one rival who had the right to share Vindex's love with me—that was Gaul our common mother.

And behold, you came, insolent daughter of conquerors, to crush underfoot all my hopes and make a slave of a free man once more! Do you still imagine that I can one day call you my sister?

BLANDINE

Yes, I believe it! My country, henceforth is his, it's yours. I am ready to leave Rome without regret, Rome thirsty under the yoke of Caesars and I will tread with joy this Gallic land which bears in its flanks the seed of the future! I, too, I understand the mission of Vindex, I, too, want him to be victorious and strong. You will see how Blandine, the Patrician girl, will share the fatigues, the perils, the struggles of those she loves. To pray for them and die with them.

KIOMARA

So you hope to leave Rome, to go to Gaul?

BLANDINE

Isn't all prepared for our departure? And once my farther is free—

KIOMARA

Your father? You mmust not even see him again.

BLANDINE

My God!

KIOMARA

It would be madness to imagine that the prisons of the Senate woulf thus give up their prey, that a Gaul, captive and condemned yesterday could cross through these jailors, these guards, the monstrous levels of subterranean cells with impunity and make the valets of Tiberius bow with a letter written by Caius.

BLANDINE

I have faith in Vindex!

KIOMARA

He promised you the impossible, he loves you so much. But, it's mno longer a question of battling lions from the Atlas mountains, and all his courage is useless. I tell you that by sparing Tiberius, you killed Vindex. Yes—you killed him!

BLANDINE

Shut up! Shut up!

KIOMARA

O the sweet and clement young girls! She got tender for a monster! She had pity for a tyrant, but she's sending her father to the executioner—she's pushing her lover under the axe!

BLANDINE

Ah, you are breaking my heart!

KIOMARA

Mine is breaking, too. But I regret Vindex less, thinking that he ruined himself for you. What have I said?Ah, hate is carrying me to crime. Avenging Gods, forget, forget my imprudence and guiklty words. Take me if you require a sacrifice, but spare Vuindex. Let him reject me, but let him live! Let him love her, let him renounce me; let him love her alone, but let him live, let him live.

ROMULUS (rushing in)

Come, come quickly.

BLANDINE

My father?

KIOMARA

Vindex?

ROMULUS

They are there—in a boat at the foot of the terrace.

BLANDINE

Saved!

KIOMARA

Flee! Ah, my reason lights up, my heart awakens, my hate is extinguished.

ROMULUS

They are waiting for you, hurry.

KIOMARA (to Blandine)

Come.

(Taking her hand effusively)

Sister!

(Blandine throws herself in Kiomara's arms.)

ROMULUS

But leave, will you!

(They leave.)

Just in time. Soldiers are invading the gardens. They are coming this way! The Praetorian Guard! By Jupiter it's the moment to use my legs again.

(He leaves, runnig. From the other direction enter Narses, Albin, followed by slaves, soldiers and courtiers.)

NARSES (to soldiers)

Scour these gardens—all the way to the shores of the Tiber and make sure no one's hidden here. I noticed tracks in the sand around here. Go!

(The soldiers disperse in various directions.)

ALBIN

It's quite a strange thing, this illness of Tiberius. What's happened?

NARSES (shrugging his shoulders)

The sinister emotions of the other night have caused such a shock and filled him with such rage that heading for Rome by forced marches, he's experienced frequent bouts of delirium, and he's fainted at least three times in the course of an hour.

ALBIN

But why's he want to stop here instead of entering the city.

NARSES

Because he suddenly remembered the prediction of Thrasyllus, his astrologer, who told him one day: "To enter Rome is to die!" He's trying trickery with the prophecy. A quite useless precaution, no doubt.

ALBIN

You think the danger swop serious?

NARSES

Tiberius is clinging to life with all his strength, but I suppose he's quite ready to go render his accounts to Minos. All the same, let's continue to serve him blindly because Tiberius is one of those monsters to whom obedience is due until has last breath.

ALBIN

That's wise reasoning. I've seen him revive so many times.

NARSES

Here he is—look!

ALBIN

Yes, he's truly a sick man

NARSES

Beware the claws of agony. They will be terrible.

(Tiberius enters and pushes away the guards who support him.)

TIBERIUS

Let me walk by myself or they'll say I cannot support myself, won't they? I feel better, much better. You see plainly I hold myself straight, and that I don't stagger.

(He falls on a bench. Aside)

It's death.

(aloud to Narses)

Didn't you tell me there were many Gauls in this suburb?

NARSES

Yes, Caesar.

TIBERIUS

In that case, I will be marvelously placed on this terrace to see the fire and the carnage.

(aside)

Will I have the time? Yes, yes.

(aloud)

Approach, Narses—all approach. Draw your swords. Light your torches, Because I want—I order that—

(aside)

O atrocious pain! o terrifying deterioration. My tongue is confused, my eyes veiled, My heart is extinguished. This crowd that's here—which spies with curiosity—doubtless with joy—my pallor, my shivers, my anguish! Stand up, Tiberius, on your feet! Make a supreme effort and dismiss them as master.

(aloud)

Leave!

(Everyone moves away.)

They fear me and obey me still. If I could struggle against the illness, remain this way a long while, become once more, through strength of will, the Tiberius of yesterday!—No, it's impossible, it's necessary that I fall back—broken. I feel as if a hand which bends me in its clasp of iron, which paralyzes me and crushes me. I feel as if a breath petrifies my face, and freezes my blood in my veins. To what invisible being belongs this breath and this hand? Is there then a power which nothing can disarm or weaken? All the while, denying the gods I've often thought, perhaps there was only one. Is Death that God?

(Caligula enters excitedly and throws himself at Tiberius' feet.)

CALIGULA

Caesar!

TIBERIUS

You, in Rome? Without my order?

CALIGULA

Pardon me, my uncle. Hardly had you left Capri when I dreamed some misfortune had befallen you. So I came, despite my wound.

TIBERIUS

He's got an excellent heart. All the same it seems that this wound was not most dangerous. Well, my child, you are going to reign.

CALIGULA

My uncle! My uncle!

(he bursts into tears.)

TIBERIUS

Mercy, control your sorrow and don't soften me with your tears. You see plainly this ring? I have only to pass it onto your finger for you to take my place.

Come on—give me your hand.

(Caius excitedly gives his hand.)

What urgency!

CALIGULA (aside)

Clumsy!

(aloud)

I only know how to obey.

TIBERIUS

Docile like a young girl. It holds much, this ring. I shall have great trouble parting with it. Still, it has to be ceded. To say that this suffices to govern Rome, to possess the supreme power. Your hand, I tell you—no, wait a bit, yet. I will give it to you later.

Soon—soon.

CALIGULA (aside)

O fever of waiting.

TIBERIUS

It's suitable that I first make you a paternal speech! Look you, Caius—once you shall be master.

CALIGULA (aside)

He's getting weaker and weaker.

TIBERIUS

Once you are master—eh, what a whirlwind, what flames, what abysses—

CALIGULA (aside)

Why, he's going to die.

TIBERIUS

What are you doing here? What are you asking? Get out! Leave me alone. I'm keeping my ring. I'm holding on to it. I don't want to separate myself from it, to have it, it will be necessary to open my fingers by force, break my fingers, perhaps.

CALIGULA

Well, since I must—

(Caligula seizes Tiberius hand and tries to snatch the ring.)

TIBERIUS (struggling, exhausted)

Ah!

CALIGULA (snatching the ring)

I've got it!

TIBERIUS

My ring! My ring! Ah, it's you who've taken it from me!

Give it back to me.

CALIGULA

Never!

TIBERIUS

So I know you at last!

CALIGULA

Not completely yet. Here!

(knocking Tiberius over)

Rome for me! Death for you!

TIBERIUS

Assassin! Help! Help!

CALIGULA

They will get here too late.

TIBERIUS

No.

(He stands up and gets loose with a supreme effort.)

To me! To me!

(All run in, including Vindex, Romulus, Narses, Nerva, Kiomara and Blandine.)

CALIGULA (aside)

I am lost.

NARSES

Caesar calls us.

TIBERIUS

Yes—for you to hear me name my successor. Listen, tribunes, aediles, consulars, citizens, soldiers—I choose as my successor—

(He stops abruptly)

NARSES

Name him, Caesar, name him, give us a master before ascending to Olympus. Rome waits, respectful and submissive.

TIBERIUS

My successor—

ALL

Speak, Tiberius, speak

TIBERIUS (pointing to Caligula)

Here he is!

CALIGULA

Me!

TIBERIUS (low to Caligula)

Yes, because if I hate you, I hate the human race morem and you alone can make Tiberius missed!

(aside, leaning on the terrace.)

Miserable city, infamous city, cursed city, whose sight gives death. To you, this master, while waiting for the one who will make an immense fire-storm of you.

(Vindex, Nerva, Romulus, Kiomara and Blandine are pushed forward, surrounded by guards.)

NARSES

Caesar, here are your prisoners.

TIBERIUS

Ah, shall I then be able to shed yet more blood? That woman—all—I intend—rage—anathema!

(His tongue becomes confused little by little, he makes only inarticulate sounds, then, exhaling a final rale, he falls over.)

CALIGULA

Romans, Tiberius is dead.

ALL

Long live Caligula!

VINDEX (low to Kiomara)

I actually said that Tiberius belongs only to God.

NARSES

(pointing to the prisoners)

What does Caesar order?

CALIGULA

(after silence, hesitating)

Let them live and let them go free.

(aside)

A bit of clemency at the beginning of a reign always produces a fine effect. Tiberius even began that way.!

(aloud)

Let there be no more fear nor mourning in Rome. I publicly cast into the fire all the proscription lists of the defunct emperor.

(Noisy applause)

(aside)

I'll take care to copy them first.

VINDEX (to Romulus)

Are you still leaving with us?

ROMULUS

Leave—when we have a new Emperor who's going to give us a whole month of parties? You cannot think of it. Goodbye, Barbarian.

VINDEX

Goodbye, Citizen of Rome.

(aside)

Incorrigible race. Brennus might be at their walls, they would run to games at the Circus!

CALIGULA (aside, eyes fixed on Rome)

All this is finally mine! More still! The universe, the immensity.

(low to Nerva)

Cast something over this dead man, will you!

(Nerva unhooks his cape and covers Tiberius.)

Now, I am all for my dear people!

(More applause.)

ROMULUS

Friends, let us bear Caesar in triumph.

ALL

Yes! Yes!

KIOMARA (to Vindex)

Brother, Gaul will be free! To you the sword that strikes!

BLANDINE

And the cross that forgives.

(Caligula is carried out with demonstrations of the most frantic enthusiasm.)

ALL

To the Capitol! To the Capitol!

CURTAIN

www.ingramcontent.com/pod-product-compliance
Lightning Source LLC
LaVergne TN
LVHW041622070426
835507LV00008B/399